LIBRARY AUTOMATION

MUHAMMAD RIAZ

ATLANTIC PUBLISHERS & DISTRIBUTTORS

Published by
ATLANTIC PUBLISHERS AND DISTRIBUTORS
B-2, Vishal Enclave, New Delhi - 27
Phone: 5413460

Sales office
4215/1, Ansari Road, Darya Ganj
New Delhi - 110002
Phone : 3273880

Typeset at
APD Computer Graphics
B-2, Vishal Enclave, N. Delhi - 27

Printed in india at
Mehra Offset Press
New Delhi

CONTENTS

List Of Figures And Tables

Introduction

Today we are living in information age. The phenomenal progress achieved by most of the industrialised countries of the world following second world war has been primarily due to the advancement made in the realm of science and technology. As a result the world saw an incredible growth of literature which eventually caused 'Information Explosion'. The conventional library methods including some dated mechanical systems used for the organization and retrieval of information failed bitterly in exercising control over the information explosion. This gave great impetus to the advent and use of computers in all walks of life.

As the computer facilities began to proliferate and became cost-effective, the library administrators started thinking in term of utilizing computers to help process unprecedented flood of literature. Libraries were quick to observe that manual practices were no longer desirable to cope with the increasing amount of reading materials received. Also the rapid growth in the number and diversity of users, and the demand for better and more personal methods played important role in changing library operational outlook. The old manual library methods were deemed as increasingly inadequate, slow, costly, difficult to use, frustrating and incapable of providing the kind and standard of service librarians wanted to render in accordance with the expectations of readers.

Simultaneously the computer technology was fast improving, thereby creating attraction for the library planner and administrators. The last two decades have specifically witnessed tremendous progress in the field of computers and telecommunication. Most recently the use of tiny silicon chip in computer technology is helping in manipulating information making millions of decisions or calculations in seconds. The old concept that computer cannot think is almost changed. It is held that the computer of silicon technology can give judgments just like any other expert human being. It is termed as Expert System or Artificial Intelligence. Memory devices with unimaginable storage capacity are getting cheaper. Floppy disk, CD-ROM and Magnetic Bubble Devices (MBD) are heavily used for information storage in libraries etc. All these events are causing an evolution in the concept of library practice.

The decade 1980 is especially significant in the field of library automation. It prompted many Librarians to adopt computer technique to solve their library problems. The computer can now perform a variety of activities such as, circulation control; acquisition; cataloguing; bibliographic processing; serials control; searching and retrieving information; rearranging and formatting data, printing out information; changing the content or structure of information at intervals of time etc.

A large number of books on computer-based library system or library automation have been published and are available to the readers. But each book has been written in its own way. The librarians or the library science students who do not have background knowledge of library automation or computer-based library systems are found to be facing difficulty in comprehending the basics of the subject. The intention to write this book is to place before the reader a lucid and a simple account of the fundamentals of library automation. Therefore, every effort has been made to avoid jargon in order to make the study interesting and attractive.

As James Rice says, the librarians need not become computer experts in the area of internal operation or processing of the computer, but they should become some knowledgeable about the central processing hardware, operating system software, application software and some peripheral equipment. The work therefore does not attempt to explain or explore the inner mechanism of computer nor does it review the duties and functions of programmers, system analysts or the computer consultants. These activities are the domain of computer experts. The book concentrates on the relevance of computer to library activities.

The book is not a research work in itself: it is derivative study based on the latest available sources such as: (1) James Rice: Introduction to Library Automation, 1989. (2) Lucy A. Tedd: An Introduction to computer-based Library System, 1984. (3) William Saffady: Introduction to Automation for Librarians, 1984. (4) Libraries in the Age of Automation. Other sources consulted are given at the end of each chapter for further study on the subject.

The book begins with a short chapter reviewing the history of computer starting from the period when computing was done by mechanical means in the beginning of seventeenth century. It traces the use of storing data on punched cards in 1800s and step by step records the march of five generations of computer age. Chapter 2 is devoted to hardware aspects and discusses the functions and sub-units of Central Processing Unit (CPU). After elaborating different methods of processing, it throws some light on the mainframe, mini and microcomputers explaining the capacity of their work and relative use in libraries.

Chapter 3 deals with the software of computers. System software and application software are introduced in lucid manner. It ends by reviewing essentials of software documentation. Chapter 4 covers a wide variety of input/output peripherals, Optical Recognition Devices, Computer Output Microfilm (COM) and reviews almost all kinds of auxiliary storage media and devices in use. Chapter 5 elucidates a number of definitions of automation in historical perspective and elaborates its modern sense and connotations. Need for library automation is identified. Computer applications in various library activities are outlined for quick reference.

Chapter 6 demonstrates computer-based circulation systems including offline and online practices and procedures. Chapter 7 describes offline and online cataloguing systems and procedures. It briefly explains MARC-I, MARC-II and their uses. In-house cataloguing procedure is also fully explained.

Chapter 8 narrates what kinds of automated reference services are being provided to library users. Computer-based bibliographic, non-bibliographic, and textual/numeric databases are manifestly explained. It introduces online information retrieval service. Some world famous bibliographic search services are discussed. Tymnet, Telenet, electronic document delivery systems are identified. Chapter 9 examines the complete range of automated acquisitions and the ordering of reading materials in library.

Chapter 10 is concerned with the automated serial control system and explains in detail its various subsystems. International Serials Control Systems (ISCS), CODEN, International Serial Data System (ISDS) and CONSER are briefly discussed. It also reviews the contributions of various subscription agencies which are operating online for the benefit of libraries.

Marriage of computer with telecommunication, and satellite communication as well as their actual and potential use in library operations are elaborately explained in chapter 11. This chapter starts by introducing the use of word processors, micrographics and reprographics in libraries. It includes topics such as technology of online services, videotex and teletext services, telefacsimile, microfacsimile, teleconferencing, computerized teleconferencing, and electronic mail etc. The potential use of satellite communication in library practices has been briefly reviewed.

Chapter 12 provides sufficient guidelines for the planning and implementation of computer-based library system. Since library automation is a major undertaking which requires positive operational justification, it examines in some detail its pros and cons and the potential problems that might emerge as a result of blindly introducing computer in libraries. It also identifies some alternative means of satisfying the library's information management needs. The need for staff training, users orientation, and finally some evaluation methods are vividly discussed.

The representation in this book is aimed at self-study and it would be useful for practicing librarians, library and information science students, the teachers and all those engaged in information handling tasks and activities.

The author is indebted to all those whose works have been used and quoted in this book. He would also like to thank Prof. Dr. Nazir Ahmed, King Abdulaziz University, Jeddah, Saudi Arabia, Mr. Usman Ahmed Danish, Assistant Prof. Allama Iqbal Open University, Islamabad and Mr. Rafiq Ahmed, Chief Reference Librarian, American Centre, Islamabad for their advice and immense help they rendered in producing this work.

Lastly the author does not claim to be an authority on the subject. It is an attempt to introduce the subject in a simple, and readable form drawing upon the latest sources available in the area of library automation for the professionals working in Pakistan and abroad.

CHAPTER 1

The History Of Computers

Computing by mechanical means dates back to ancient time. The abacus has been used for thousands of years in China and Japan. This device satisfied most calculating requirements until the development of western societies which required assistance in managing large volumes of calculations. This led to the introduction of logarithms. These were developed by John Napier who published his first long tables in 1614. These devices provided methods by which multiplication and division could be achieved through addition and subtraction. In the 1620s William Oughtred developed the slide-rule based on the concept of logarithms. Both these inventions were widely used until the development of small electronic calculators in the late 1960s.

Two further significant development took place in the seventeenth century. The first was the production of a mechanical calculator by Blaise Pascal in 1647. The second was a more effective calculator produced by Gottried Leibnitz in 1694 which performed multiplication and division. Although both the machines produced correct results, there were considerable problems still unsolved.

The work done by Charles Babbage in the nineteenth century is considered the next major development in the history of computer design. Babbage in 1821 designed his 'Difference Engine' and in 1832 his 'Analytical Engine', which is generally recognized as the milestone signifying the start of the computer age. Babbage's plans called for the machine to work from a set of instructions. These operating instructings would be stored in an appropriate sequence on punched cards. The Analytical Engine would also store information inside the machine so that the complex processing of numbers could be performed. From this perspective; it is clear that the ideas of internal memory, central processing, and storage of information on punched cards were actually conceived far ahead of their time. (Rowntree)

In the late 1800s, the idea of storing data on punched card was introduced in a tabulating machine. Herman Hollerith had developed this machine in 1883. Demographic data were stored on these cards and processed by the machine. This device was used in United States in 1890 census. (J. Rice)

By the end of nineteenth century two key engineering concepts: a machine operated by set of instructions and data represented in code on cards had been established. Babbage's devices were purely mechanical whereas Hollerith's tabulator used electric power. In 1911 Hollerith's Tabulating Machine Company, which was founded in 1896, merged with two other companies, and in 1924 they became the International Business Machine Corporation (IBM).

In 1937, Howard Aiken, a Harvard graduate student in physics developed plans for an automatic digital calculator called Mark 1. Later IBM helped him making a large Automatic Sequence Controlled Calculator. It was a electromechanical device which performed automatically from stored instructions.

During the coming years, scientists designed more powerful and more reliable computers. This involved a trend away from mechanical designs towards electronic designs. In 1946, a computer using vacuum tubes was built at the University of Pennsylvania named ENIAC. It is often called the first fully automatic electronic digital computer. One might not believe that the first computer weighted 30 tons, contained 18000 vacuum tubes, 70,000 resisters, 10,000 capacitors and 600 switches and cost amounted to U.S.$ 500,000. Still it was not considered reliable and would fail frequently. Research in the field of computing accelerated tremendously in the next four decades. Major advances however occurred in the following areas:

1. The ability to store greater amounts of information in the computer itself.
2. Speed of processing.
3. Miniaturization.
4. The ability to use instructions based on natural language.
5. Auxiliary storage media such as floppy disk or CD-Rom Disk etc.
6. The ability of the computer to interact with a variety of input/output remote terminals.
7. Marriage of computer with telecommunication and satellite communication.

Historically, the evolution of computers is divided into five generations. These are reviewed here in some detail.

FIRST GENERATION OF COMPUTERS.

The first truly electronic computer was the Electronic Numerical Integrator and calculator (ENIAC). It was completed in 1946 by Mauchly and Eckert at the University of Pennsylvania. It used high speed vacuum tube switching devices and had very small memory. It was basically designed to calculate the trajectories of missiles.

Commercial production of stored program electronic computers began in the early 1950s. One of the early computers of this type was UNIVAC I built by Univac division of Remington Rand. This computer also used vacuum tubes. As vacuum tubes used filaments as a source of electrons, they had a limited life.

During this period, computer programming was mainly done in machine language. Assembly language was invented in the early fifties. The initial applications was in the field of science and engineering.

THE SECOND GENERATION.

A big revolution in electronics took place with the advent of transistors by Bardeen, Brattain and Shockley in 1946. The first generation of computer had been characterized by the use of vacuum tubes in the electric circuity. This second generation used transistors instead of vacuum tubes. Transistors made of germanium semi-conductor material were highly reliable compared to tubes since transistors had no filament to burn. They occupied less space and used only a tenth of power required by tubes, and were ten times faster and cheaper than those using tubes.

During this period magnetic cores were invented. They were used to construct large random access memories. Magnetic disk storage was also developed during this period. High level languages such as Fortran, Cobol, Algol and Snobol were also developed during this generation.

THE THIRD GENERATION.

The third generation began in 1965. The germanium transistors were replaced by silicon transistors. This generation is characterized as "Integrated Circuits" computers. Integrated circuits, circuits consisting of transistors, registers, and capacitors grown on a single chip of silicon eliminating wired interconnection between components emerged on scene.

Significants improvements were brought about in the design of magnetic core memories, and magnetic disk technology. The combined effect of high memory, powerful CPU and large disk memories led to the development of time shared operating systems. Many important online systems became feasible. Airline reservation, interactive query systems were developed. Integrated data base management systems emerged.

High level languages improved. Fortran IV and optimizing Fortran compilers were developed. COBOL 68 was standardized. PL/I of IBM emerged and was a powerful language. The improvements in this period (1965-75) were substantial. This generation probably ended by 1975.

THE FOURTH GENERATION.

The fourth generation of computer, in which we live is identified by the advent of the microprocessor chip. A large and a Very Large Scale Integrated circuits (VLSI) packing about 50000 transistors in a chip is featured. Magnetic core memories have been replaced by semiconductor memories. The emergence of the microprocessor has led to two directions in computer development. One is the emergence of powerful personal computers. Computer cost has come down tremendously enabling anyone to buy it. Floppy disk provides a low cost high capacity back up peripheral memory.

The other direction of development is the decentralisation of computer organization. Individual microprocessor controls for terminals and peripheral devices have allowed the CPU to concentrate on processing the main program. Networks of computers and distributed computer systems have been developed. Disk memories have become very large - CD-ROM being the latest invention. A significant development in software is the development of concurrent programming languages. Such languages are important to program distributed systems and real time systems. Another important development is interactive graphic devices and language interfaces to graphic systems. Finally this generation has seen the coming of age of time shared interactive systems.

THE FIFTH GENERATION.

What the fifth generation will contribute, is still unclear. In Japan research is making assault to develop artificial intelligence capable of accommodating functions such as intelligent conversation and inference functions employing knowledge bases. It would be a sublime achievement in the realm of computation research.

Expert systems are part of the broader science of Artificial Intelligence Systems, i.e. the fifth generation computer research program as stated above. By Expert system means the computers that perform tasks that are usually performed by experts. These expert systems are quite new, highly sophisticated taking the users far beyond the limited functions of data processing storage or retrieval into the most exciting new area of decision making in the specific field of application. Although restricted in the type of tasks they can perform, demonstrate expertise in solving suitable problems. For instance robots are widely used in industrial sector. They keep the wheels of industry moving at all times. Once he is given programmed instructions, the robot's mechanical arms do the work which normally require several pairs of human hands. The new robots (about 8000 are employed in the world) are not a simple mechanical arms, but intelligent, thinking devices that can 'see' what they are doing. Today robots can only 'see' but tomorrow they might 'hear' and then further develop the senses of touch and taste.

Select Bibliography

Fundamentals of Computing. Edited by G. Rowntree. Manchester: NCC Pub. 1987.

Kent, Allen. Information Analysis and Retrieval. New York: Wiley-Becker Heyes, 1971.

Metropolis, N. et. al. A History of Computing in the Twentieth Century. New York: Academic Press, 1980.

Rajaraman, V. Fundamentals of Computer. New-Delhi: Prentice Hall of India, 1985.

Reynolds Dennis. Library Automation: Issues and Applications. New York: R. R. Bowker, 1985.

Rice James. Introduction to Library Automation. Littleton: Libraries Unlimited, 1984.

CHAPTER 2

Hardware Aspects

The term hardware refers to the physical equipment of a computing system. In the early days the term hardware was used to denote mechanical devices such as analytical engine devised in 1833 to perform calculatings automatically using punched cards. In the 1940s the first electronic computer i.e. ENIAC, came into being. The equipment is known as hardware.

A computer system consists of three major groups of components. These are: hardware or equipment, software or the programs, and the data or information which the hardware and software processes, stores, retrieves or manipulate. From hardware viewpoint a computer system may consist of several hundred thousand to several million electronic components. For a simplified description, a computer hardware components are generally divided into two broad groups:

(i) The computer itself. It is also called the central processor, the central processing unit (CPU) or graphically the mainframe.

(ii) The peripheral (input/output) devices. Peripheral means the devices which are associated with the CPU. They may be located around it; but are not a part of it. If a given peripheral is connected to the central processing unit it is said to be operating online, if not connected, it is called offline. (For diagram of a total computer system see figure 2.1).

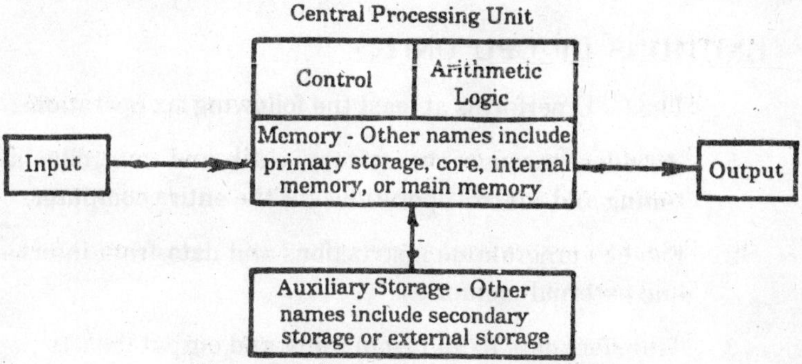

Fig. 2.1 A Total Computer System

This categorization is applicable almost to other types of information processing equipment including word processing systems, micrographic systems, and facsimile transmission systems. The various peripheral devices are design to perform one or more of the specialized information processing tasks such as input, output and storage.

CENTRAL PROCESSING UNIT (CPU).

Central Processing Unit is the central and the main unit of the computer. All manipulation and arrangements, arithmetic and logic operations or processing of data is performed in this unit. Sometimes CPU is referred to as the computer itself. It normally works under the control of a program supplied to it by the computer programmer. And a program is a set of instructions which explains the complete logic of processing and direct the CPU to function. (See Figure 2.2).

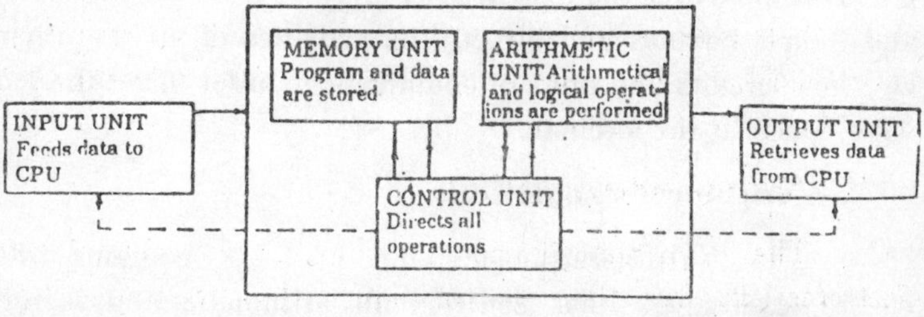

Fig. 2.2 Central Processing Unit (CPU)

FUNCTIONS OF CPU UNIT

The CPU performs at least the following six operations:

1. Provides, through the system, clock and controller all timing and control operations for the entire computer.
2. Fatches programme instructions and data from internal and external memories.
3. Transfers data to and from input and output devices.
4. Decodes instruction by assigning input code values to corresponding binary register values.
5. Manipulate data.
6. Alters the flow of instruction execution from signals generated by input and output devices.

The CPU contains the following three sub-units:

1. Control Unit.
2. Arithmetic/Logic Unit
3. Storage Unit

1. Control Unit.

The Control Unit contains circuitry, that with electrical signals directs and coordinates the entire input processing and output operations. It examines the instructions contained in the program, and sends out the electronic signals which instigate the required operations. In other words, the function of the control unit is to interpret the instructions given to it by the operator, and then schedules and directs the activities of all the other electrical circuits and units of equipment in order to get the job done. It acts as the foreman.

2. Arithmetic/Logic Unit.

The Arithmetic/Logic Unit (A.L.U.) contains the electronic circuitry that controls all arithmetic and logical operations. It functions as the mill or processor which, under the leadership of the control unit, operates on the information given to it and perform all of the logical testing and processing required. It can perform arithmetic operations such as addition and multiplication as well as many logical operations such as comparisons, and the extractions of selected portions of a string of number or characters.

3. Storage Unit.

The store or main memory of the computer holds items of information for as long as they are needed. The main store is used to store information currently being processed. The information may take the form of instructions constituting a program to be executed, or data in which that program is to operate.

The storage of a computer is not unlimited; it holds some maximum quantity of data. These data may be in the form of characters - usually, the digits 0 to 9, letter A to Z, and a number of special characters, such as *,.- + 0 $ @ # and %. The capacity of these memories is often used as a measure of the power of the computer. Storage devices are also rated by the speed with which data can be withdrawn from them.

In early computer systems magnetic cores or rings were used, but now silicon chips are used which are much cheaper. The most common such memory can be written as well as read. There are four types of main memories, namely ROM, PROM, EPROM, and RAM. A ROM or "Read Only Memory" refers to the memory composed of a chip with specific circuits designed to contain programs and data that are permanently recorded into the memory and cannot be changed by the user. If the program requires changes then the entire chip must be replaced and redesigned.

A PROM or "Programmable Read Only Memory" is also used for specific application but does not need to be manipulated in large quantities. Rather simple chips may be programmed by breaking connects between circuits holding the common value of all "Os" or all "IS".

EPROM or "Electronically Programmable Read Only Memory" is constructed not by breaking circuits between values. It may be programmed over an over again without being replaced. It is most expensive of all the memory types.

A RAM or "Random Access Memory" is a general purpose memory used by the Central Processing Unit (CPU) to store data and programs. Random Access memory means that in order to know a value contained in the middle of the chip, there is no need to examine each circuit starting at the beginning and going forward one circuit at a time. Rather, the locations for the specific circuit values may be calculated and accessed randomly i.e. directly.

The individual units performing the above three functions are the sub-units of the CPU. They may be housed in a single physical unit or in more than one physical units. Generally, the Arithmetic/Logic Unit, the Control Unit and some basic memory or primary storage are located in a single physical unit. Additional memory or auxiliary storage is attached to it in modules in additional physical units.

Backing Store.

The information that is not currently being processed is kept on some form of backing storage device. This store actually provides the filing system for the computer and consists of magnetic tape reels. But in most mainframe computers backing stores magnetic disc is used. The input, output and backing store units together are called peripherals i.e. those which are outside and not part of main equipment.

ANALOG VS. DIGITAL COMPUTERS.

Analog computer accepts information for processing in physical form in terms of weight, volume, electric current etc. It can translate temperature, flow, speed altitude, voltage and other physical variable into related electrical quantities, and for this purpose it uses electrical equivalent circuits. It performs calculations on the incoming information according to a predetermined pattern which is usually represented by mechanical, electro-mechanical or electronic units. The computer is usually built to satisfy a particular requirement and is mostly used for scientific work. They are not suitable for library purpose.

Digital computer accepts information in a unitary form, i.e. letter, symbols and numbers. These may represent anything the computer user wants. All calculations or processing of the incoming data is done on the digital form, and the results are printed-out in conventional letters, symbols or numbers. It operates at a terrific high speed. The digital computers are general purpose computers suitable for information processing and are particularly suited to libraries.

METHODS OF PROCESSING

Three methods are identified by which information can be processed by a computer system. These are:

(1) Batch Processing (offline)
(2) Real-Time Processing (online)
(3) Remote Job Entry Processing.

1. Batch Processing.

The terms "batch processing" and real-time processing are commonly used to describe modes of data processing. Batch processing is a method of processing data in blocks or batches and prepared for computer input as a single unit. This means that one program is finished before another is started and programs are placed in a queue, or batched ready to be processed. Batch processing present problems for a librarian. First there will be a time delay before the results of a program are obtained and secondly direct access to the computer is out of question. Therefore interaction with the program or data file is not possible. Batch processing is one of the oldest and least costly mode of running programs. Stephen Flowers outlines features of batch processing as follows:-

1. Information held in batch-processing files is always out of date, since it is only as recent as the last time a batch of transactions was submitted for processing. This may not be important for some applications.

2. Batch processing lends itself to the processing of large numbers of similar transactions which require careful checking.

3. Transactions are passed to the computer centre for processing by specialist computer staff, with output being returned to the user to be stored or used at will.

4. It is easy to schedule processing at set times and therefore easier to organise work on a large computer with many competing users.

5. It is easier to control the input and processing of data with batch processing than with the on-line or distributed methods.

6. Batch processing has been declining in use as on-line and distributed or remote job entry processing have been installed for applications requiring up-to-date information or decentralised computing facilities.

2. Real-time Processing.

Online processing is often called real time processing. In this system the terminals have a direct connection (or online) with the computer in such a way that data can be fed to the processor directly. The term 'real-time' means 'as they accur'. In this system, there is no need to present data in machine-readable media such as punched cards or paper tape or magnetic tape because intake data are processed on arrival at the computer system and summarised instantaneously on the display screen as output.

Real-time processing derives from the fact that the computer can deliver the necessary output at the sametime the actual transaction is completed. In real-time processing many remote stations may be connected directly by the high-speed communication system with the central processor, and several stations may be operating at a time. In libraries a real-time circulation system has instant up-to-date circulation information available and is ready to complete the next transaction at once. Flowers features online processing as follows:

Features of on-line processing.

1. No delay in the processing of information, so that output can be received back as soon as processing is complete.

2. Associated with fairly low volumes of input and output from many separate locations combining to produce a high level of processing at the central computer.

3. Master files will always be up-to-date and reflect the current state of the business.

4. The system will usually enable on-line enquiries to be made to the master file, requesting information on customer account balances etc.

5. It is harder to control the quality of data input, since non-specialist users may be entering the data.

6. Increasingly used - it has been estimated that perhaps 75% of all processing may be done on-line by 1990.

3. Remote Job Entry.

When batch and online processing is linked through an online terminal or typewriter like machine in order to enter a program into the queue of programs to be batch processed by the computer, this is called Remote Job Entry. When the computer has completed the program the resultant files may be interrogated online from the terminal. (Tedd).

BITS, BYTES AND WORDS.

Binary digit or Bit is the basic unit of information storage used in all digital computer systems. In simple words computer memories use binary symbols (0. and 1) due to the nature of electronic circuits used in them. A bit is expressed by a high or low electrical voltage. Letters, numbers, punctuation marks, special symbols, etc. are represented by a specific combination or binary symbols for use with computers. The information (or input) to a computer consists only of symbols. Some of these symbols represent instructions and the rest is data.

Bits can be group together to form a byte and a byte normally consists of 8 bits. A byte is often used to represent a character. And a "Character" is any letter, numeral, punctuation, mark or other symbol found in data. Byte being a unit of information consisting of a fixed number of bits, is treated as an entry for encoding a single letter, number or symbol. A number of coding schemes have been developed. For example the American Standard Code for Information Interchange (ASCII) uses 01100001 for the letter 'a' EBCDIC which stands for Extended Binary Code Decimal Interchange Code is another example. It is established by IBM and used extensively in the IBM 360/370 models as well as in the 4300 model series. This scheme of coding uses eight bits to represent a single character. The letter A for instance is represented by 1100001.

A computer's capacity-that of both primary memory and secondary storage devices-is measured in bytes and expressed as a number followed by the symbol K or KB. 1KB stands for 1024 bytes. A computer having 128K of main memory can store 128 times 1024 bytes or characters.

While Byte is used to express the memory or storage capacity of CPU, the computer capacity is described in "words", a measure that denotes the number of bites the control unit can retrieve from the primary memory at one time. For example, an 8-bit word computer, can access 8 bits or one byte (one character) at a time. The word lengths of available computing devices range from 8 to 64-bits, although most of the machines installed in libraries have 8-or 16-bit word-length capacity. A word is thus a string of binary digits, which is treated as a single unit of data by a computer.

A computer's word can be used either for storing information or for storing instructions. A basic instruction is made up of two parts; firstly the operation code which describes what operation is to be performed and secondly the address (or addresses) of the data word (or words) which would be used for operation.

CLASSIFICATION OF COMPUTERS

Depending upon physical size, processing power, intended application and price, computers are generally categorized as mainframes, minicomputers and microcomputers. The differences among the three categories are ill-defined since the minis have become as fast and powerful as many mainframes and micros are challenging the minis. However the general range of their capabilities can be identified.

Mainframe.

Mainframe or full-sized computers are very powerful and special-purpose equipment. They are designed for scientific or other research applications requiring extremely rapid execution of high volume of complex calculations. This type of computer is typically acquired by an organization such as university, research and industrial establishment to provide them a centralized service for a wide variety of purposes. Mainframes have a lot of storage facilities, enable the information to be input and output in a variety of ways. They can support a large number of terminals, provide a range of special features for the programmer and so on. They are available in different sizes. At the low end of this product group, the small full-size computers are virtually, in some cases less powerful than the largest minicomputers. Their main memory capacities range from 512K to several megabytes. They access 32-bit words and their operation speeds are typically measured in microseconds (millionths of a second). On the other end of the full size computer group are so-called Supercomputers, very powerful, special-purpose machines designed for scientific or other research applications requiring the very fast execution of a high volume of complex calculations. Their word size is 64 bits; their operating speeds are measured in fractions of a nanosecond (a billionth of a second). They provide main memory capacity for millions of characters.

Between these two extremes, .most full-size computers are properly identified as medium or large-scale devices designed to perform the most commonly done scientific and data processing tasks. Medium-scale computers are generally faster and support a wide range of peripheral devices than the small full-size computers. They access 64-bits words, offer several megabytes of main memory and operating speed is measured in nanoseconds. Examples of mainframe computers include the Amdhal 470 series, Honeywell 6000 series, CDC 7600 series, IBM 370 series, etc.

Full-size computers are used in U.S. by bibliographic utilities, online search services and other organizations providing automated reference and technical services to libraries (Saffady).

Minicomputers.

Produced in the late 1950s using the then technology of integrated circuits were called minicomputers. They are also available in a wide range of sizes and speeds. "Super-minis" are more powerful than some smaller full-sized computers. These are 32 bit word length machines; operating speed i.e. CPU speeds is measured in microseconds or even nanoseconds.

A typical minicomputers are with word length as 12 to 16 bits; operating speed measured in microseconds and main memory capacities of 512K to several megabytes etc.

American firm Digital Equipment Corporation has developed a variety of minicomputer such as PDP-II, DEC-10 and the VAX series. Minicomputers are acquired by individual departments such as a library or information unit and may be linked to a mainframe for the provision of extra processing requirements. Sometimes several minicomputers are linked together in order to provide a centralized computing resource within an organization.

Minicomputers are often incorporated in the turnkey systems developed for library applications. They are sometimes used to control all the input from, and output to, terminals linked to a mainframe computer. In general the speed, storage capacity, software facilities are not as great on minicomputer systems as on mainframe computers.

Microcomputer.

The mini is being increasingly challenged by microcomputer on various reasons. Microcomputers appeared in the late 1970s when microprocessors were linked with appropriate storage and input and output devices to provide a computing system. They are now capable of storing a fair amount of information and provide a variety of programming possibilities. The first microcomputers were based on microprocessors with a word length of 8 bits. Examples of 8 bit microcomputers are Apple-II and Apple-III. More recent microcomputers are based on microprocessors with a word length of 16 bits and 32 bits thus providing faster processing speeds and increased storage facilities. 16-bit and 32-bit microprocessors support longer instruction; a larger, more versatile instruction set; and large memory configurations. Among 32 bit microcomputer the IBM Personal System/2 Model 80 is most suitable for library application.

Multi-user, multi-task microcomputers hold great promise for libraries on the ground that they can accommodate several terminals and can do several jobs concurrently.

Microcomputers have also become popular for individual computer use. They are identified as "Personal Computer", or more recently as "Professional Computer" and can be used by one person. The simplest personal computers incorporate a microprocessor, random access memory circuits and a Keyboard in a single unit designed to be attached to a television monitor.

But personal computers are never recommended for use in libraries.

Saffady has pointed out that relatively few libraries and library systems have their own mainframe or full-sized computers. Many libraries have only access to full-sized computers operated by an institutional or corporate data processing centre. Although mainframe computers provide a centralized data processing facilities, a number of libraries have expressed dis-satisfaction with such arrangements mainly because of un-responsive attitude of computer centre personnel and demand direct control over computing resources. Development in electronics technology, advent of silicon chip resulting in drastic low cost, availability of microcomputers and turnkey systems etc. have further increased libraries desire to have their own computer systems.

GENERAL CHARACTERISTICS OF COMPUTER

A computer can be better understood from the various functions it can perform. But still the latest equipment lacks human intelligence and acts with its inherent limitations. Some of the interesting features of the computer are reviewed as follow:

1. Computers are built to carry out a small variety of instructions. It is not necessary to have more than about 100 distinct instructions even for a very powerful equipment.
2. Instructions are extremely simple e.g. add, subtract, read a character, write a character, compare number.
3. Most instructions are carried out in less than millionth of a second.
4. Instructions are carried out obediently with no question asked.
5. Instructions are carried out without any mistake.

Computer is like a servant who would carry out instructions obediently, uncritically at a very high speed, and without expressing any emotions. It must be understood that computers are machines which can be programmed to follow instructions; they don't have their own priorities and judgments.

Select Bibliography

Evans, C. The Making of the Micro: A History of the Computer. New York: Van Nostrand Reinhold, 1981.

Flowers,Stephen. Success in Information Processing. Suffolk: John Murray, 1988.

Fosdick, Howard. Computer Basics for Libraries and Information Scientists. Arlington, Va: Information Resources Press, 1981.

Fundamentals of Computing. Edited by Graham Rowntree. Manchester: NCC Pub. 1987.

Gorsline, G. W. Computer Organization: Hardware-Software. Englewood Cliffs, N.J. Prentice Hall, 1980.

Libraries in the Age of Automation; a Reader for the Professional Librarian. New York: Knowledge Industry Pub. 1986.

Matick, R. W. Computer Storage Systems and Technology. New York: Wiley, 1977.

Myers, G. J. Advances in Computer Architecture. 2nd ed. New York: Wiley, 1981.

Rajaraman, V. Fundamentals of Computers. New Delhi: Prentice-Hall of India, 1985.

Rice James. Introduction to Library Automation. Littleton: Libraries Unlimited, 1984.

Spencer, Donald. D. Computers and Information Processing. Columbus: Charles E. Merrill Pub. 1985.

Tedd, Lucy A. An Introduction to Computer-based Library Systems. 2nd ed. New York: John Wiley, 1984.

Walsh, M. E. Understanding Computers: What Managers and Users need to Know. New York: Wiley, 1981.

CHAPTER 3

Software Aspects

Computer are terrific problem solvers, but they can't do their work without assistance. All computer equipment including the central processing unit and all of its online and offline peripheral devices such as visual displays, magnetic disk drives, printers and data preparation devices are called hardware. This physical equipment won't work without programs that instruct and guide the operations of each device. These programs is called software; without them computer systems are as useless as a car without fuel. Tedd defines it as: "software is the general term used to describe the types of programs, or lists of instructions which are needed to enable the computer system to carry out the necessary processing." (Spencer)

Unlike different car models which can run on the same types of fuel, computer hardware cannot be run on just one kind of software. Thus software is machine-specific-what runs on one machine may not run on another system and vice versa. Whether it is on disk, cassette, magnetic tape, or plug-in modules, software is designed specifically for one type of machine and is not compatible with other hardware.

Some computer manufacturers provide total hardware and software, or turnkey systems for library applications. But more often the hardware and software are supplied separately. Therefore, the librarians interested in acquiring any computer systems have to decide what software should be purchased as well as what hardware.

TYPES OF SOFTWARE

There are basically two types of software: system software and application software. Both are essential before any useful work can be obtained from computer systems. All computer software is made up of programs.

SYSTEMS SOFTWARE.

System software means collection of those programs which enable a computer to function and control its own operation. They are routines residing in the computer's memory that help the programmer to write, test, modify or execute an applications program. This type of software makes computers easier to use because it facilitates communications between the machine and its operator or programmer. System software is further divided into three categories:

1. Operating System.
2. Utility Programs.
3. Data Base Management Systems (DBMS)

1. Operating Systems.

Modern computer hardware is highly powerful and complicated which more often creates difficult situation for the users. The operating system serves as an interface between the user and the computer. In other words it acts as intermediary between the user and the computer accepting and responding to commands submitted in a special job control language (JCL). It is a program that controls the operation of various computer resources. For example it determines which program of instructions the central processing unit works on at each point time. It allocates primary storage space to programs and data. It shifts programs and data from lower levels of storage to main storage and back again.

The Operating System (OS) is a large and complex program that determines how a particular computer's CPU accepts incoming signals, transmits ongoing signals, allocates storage space to individual use and program, control the various peripheral devices, permits access to various files of data and accomplishes other house keeping tasks. Thus the purpose of the operating system is to manage computer hardware so that it is used as efficiently as possible. For instance, a CPU operates much faster than lower levels of storage and other I/0 devices. Because of this OS resorts to multiprogramming and it interupts to keep the CPU busy. Multiprogramming has led to the use of virtual memory. The virtual storage system attempts to make internal storage appear larger than it really is through the use of an extremely fast auxiliary storage device located close to the CPU. When virtual storage is used, portion of data files and programs are moved-back and forth between it and internal storage by the operating system. Thus the operating system becomes an extremely dynamic manager of space, changing the contents of internal storage in response to the user's needs.

Operating systems are divided into single user and multi-user OS. Those operating systems designed for personal computer, handle one task only at a time, but now multitask OS are available on PC. The operating systems designed for mainframe, minicomputer, and microcomputers are capable of multiprogramming - that is maintaining two or more programs in main memory and executing two or more tasks simultaneously. The operating system is normally written by the computer manufacturer and provided with their equipment.

2. Utility Program.

Utility programs are routine programs of general nature which are often required to be used during the processing of the application systems and testing of the programs. Examples of these programs are file conversion programs like copying a card file to a magnetic tape, magnetic tape to disk, print out of magnetic tape or disk, card to print, printing the contents of the CPU memory etc. Other common utility programs are designed to sort data into a predefined sequence or to merge two or more sets of presorted data. Other programs assist in the detection and correction of errors or "bugs" faced during program testing.

Utility programs may be obtained from computer equipment manufacturers or companies specializing in software development, or may be developed by local programmers.

3. Data Base Management Systems.

The term database generally refers to a machine-readable file of bibliographic records, for example the MARC database. However in computer science the term is also used to refer to a more general shared collection of data which is used by several, often many, applications programs. The software which handles all access to such a database is known as a database management system (DBMS). The system has become a popular way of handling large files of nonnumerical data, including bibliographic information. The formal definition of data base management systems is "a data base management system allows multiple independent users to have concurrent access to a central repository of information". Tedd with reference to Kvitsand describes the components of a DBMS as under:

(1) Provides a way of describing the structure of the data.

(2) Enables existing data to be incorporated into the new database.

(3) Provides facilities for the manipulation of data from application programs.

(4) Enables the database to be maintained and updated as and when necessary.

A DBMS eliminates data redundancy. Each bibliographic record has to be entered only once as a DBMS permits access to the entire record through any of its fields. Before the development of DBMSs, one had to either create separate files for each required access approach - author, title, subject, call number etc; - or create multiple indexes to the bibliographic file at the time the data base was being developed. A DBMS provides the ability to modify- and even restructure-the database without affecting existing programs or creating new file structure. This facility is known as data independence.

The design and architecture of almost all DBMS software packages permit multiple independent users to access common data. When the same data are accessed by independent users, data are said to be "shared". Again sharing means not only that the data base can be accessed by multiple independent users, but it can also be accessed by multiple users at the same time.

A DBMS is more important when several users are working with the data base at the same time than when data are accessed serially because concurrent users can more easily interfere with each other's use of the data base. A DBMS does require the use of considerable computer resources, but this can be justified by the benefits it provides. A DBMS is most useful in an online environment with large data bases and a need for concurrency.

DBMS software are available on mainframe and minicomputer systems. ADABAS is one example of such a DBMS. Data Retrieval System (DRS) is used in US and INFO is used in the UK by various libraries. One of the most sophisticated DBMS packages available on microcomputers is MDBS-microdatabase management system. Another popular DBMS package for microcomputers is Dbase II, III & IV developed by Ashton-Tate in the US and is used by many libraries. The advent of DBMS software on microcomputer has radically resolved library problems. A number of libraries and information units in US are using standard DBMS or DMS software, and adopting their data if necessary, rather than develop special purpose programs.

The medium of communication with the computer is the computer language. Since all the computers understand the coded programs, such programs are known as the coded language. If the coded languages are machine-dependent, they are called lower level language. But there are now several machine-independent languages: they are known as higher-level language.

All computer programs are written in programming languages. System software too is written in a programming language, but the term is most commonly used in connection with application software. Three other examples of system software, i.e. assemblers, compilers and interpreters are also discussed here because they function as "Translator" of programming languages.

TYPES OF PROGRAMMING LANGUAGES.

Computers use different programming languages just as people in various parts of the world speak different languages. Programming is therefore key to successful computer use. As stated earlier, it involves writing a set of instructions in a sequence that produces a desired result when the sequence is executed by the computer. There are many different levels of programming languages (levels of coding) but they are generally organized into the following categories:

1. Machine Language.
2. Assembly Language.
3. Higher-level Language.

All programming languages except machine language are symbolic and must be translated into machine language instructions. Symbolic coding involves programming a computer to recognize instructions in a language more easily understood by the user and then translating these expressions into machine language.

1. Machine Language.

Machine language is the common language of a particular computer and does not require further modification before use. A program written in machine language is a sequence of binary numbers (I's and O's) Once the problem is identified, the programmer codes the operation using codes the computer can interpret. Basic instructions to a computer consists of operations such as add, subtract, multiply, divide, store, read, write etc.

As stated above, a machine language comprises numeric symbols and is designed for use by a computer directly without translation. Machine language consists of the total set or stock of operations instructions the machine can perform. For instance a hundred different instructions including input/out as well as arithmetical operations for handling numeric data and logical operations for handling alphanumeric data. A decimal number is converted into the corresponding binary number when the instruction is read into the CPU.

The translation of data from alphanumeric symbols to binary codes and back is done by the computer itself. The computer programmers normally write their instructions using either assembler language or a higher level language.

2. Assembly Language.

Assembly language is similar to machine language but it has been designed to facilitate human understanding. Symbols and abbreviations are used in assembly language instead of I's and O's (bits) used in machine language. Writing programs using mnemonic commands in place of binary codes has made software development process more efficient. In assembly language, it is common to use mnemonic codes in programming such as ADD, MOV (move) and STO (Store). These commands are much easier for a programmer to remember than the machine-level counterparts. Frequently used instruction sequences can be combined into a single mnemonic code.

Although easier to write, the individual instructions comprising assembly language programs are then translated into the binary-coded machine language that the computer requires. This translation is performed automatically by the computer using a special program called is assembler. The assembly routine reads the symbolic program from input such as punched cards, translates the mnemonic operation codes to machine operation codes and assigns memory locations for storing instruction and data. The assembler outputs a machine-language program.

The advantage of the symbolic coding and assembly program compared with coding directly in machine coding are as follow:

1. Coding is easier, since the programmer can use easy-to-remember mnemonic and symbolic address tags.

2. If a program is changed later on or if two programs are combined, machine language programming would require extensive checking to prevent incompatible memory location use. Programs written in symbolic code are merely reassembled to provide a reassignment of memory locations.

3. The assembly routine provides diagnostic routines to detect errors.

Since assembly language is akin to machine language, it is most often used in those situations where the programmer requires very close control over the internal operation of CPU. Although it is suitable for writing applications programs, assembly language is relatively slow to use from the standpoint of the programmer. While they differ in ease of use, machine language and assembly language are collectively called lower-level languages. As a result, applications software is now usually written in one of the so-called higher-level programming languages such as COBOL FORTRAN etc.

3. Higher-level Languages.

In contrast to machine and assembly languages which are machine-dependent, higher-level languages are relatively machine-independent. Higher level languages are closer to natural language. Many higher-level language allow the use of English-language commands. Higher language programs are easier, faster and less expensive to develop than those written in machine or assembly language. The higher level languages are often called application languages. A variety of such languages has been developed: the most popular are FORTRAN, COBOL PL/1, BASIC and Pascal.

Examples of Higher-Level Languages:

1. **Algol 60:** Algol 60 was designed by an international Committee in 1960 for the solution of scientific problems, but has been used for some library applications. It has influenced the design of nearly all more modern language (Tedd).

2. **Basic:** Basic, or Beginner's all-purpose symbolic instruction code, was designed by J. Kemeny and T.E. Kurtz of Dartmouth College, New Jersey to be an easy-to-learn language suitable for beginners. Nearly all microcomputers have facilities for writing Basic programs and although it is a fairly simple language it has been used for a number of library applications.

3. **Cobol:** Cobol stands for Common Business Oriented Language and was designed in the late 1950s. Most library applications have more in common with business than science and so COBOL has been used for programming many library systems.

4. **Comit:** Comit has string manipulation facility like SNOBOL. Being a higher-level language, it is relatively easy to learn. It is a special purpose language and can work in a limited field. COMIT is basically designed for use in studies of mechanical translation of human language. SNOBOL IV and COMIT-the string processing program languages are used only where highly complex bibliographic records are to be manipulated.

5. **Fortran:** Fortran stands for Formula Translator and was designed, mainly by people working at IBM, in the US in the mid-1950s. There have been several versions of the language accepted as standard by the American National Standards Institute (ANSI). During the early 1970s the standard was known as Fortran IV and the current standard is known as Fortran 77. Fortran has been used for many library applications programs.

6. **Pascal:** This was designed by Nicklaus Wirth, in Zurich, in the early 1970s. It is gaining favour amongst some as a better language for beginners than Basic. It is available on many microcomputer systems.

7. **PL/1:** This stands for Programming Language One, which was designed in the mid-1960s to combine the file-handling properties of Cobol, the numerical features of Fortran and the Structure of Algol 60. (Tedd).

8. **Snobol:** Stands for string-oriented symbolic language. This program language has string-manipulation facility as in PL/1. It is the unique program language that provides complete facilities for the manipulation of strings of characters and capability in program compilation and generation of symbolic operations. The revised version of SNOBOL is SNOBOL IV. It can perform general data processing functions.

Higher-level languages are either procedure-oriented or problem oriented. Most are procedure-oriented, designed for writing logical sequences of instructions. COBOL is typical example. Problem-oriented languages are designed for solving specific types of problems.

Higher-level languages offer some advantages such as: (1) require fewer instructions to accomplish a task than assembler languages, (2) provide instructions specifically oriented towards the problem at hand, and (3) tend to be relatively "portable" meaning that a program written in PASCAL for an IBM mainframe computer is likely to work on a DEC minicomputer (assuming that both have PASCAL compilers) and with only minor changes may also work on an Apple microcomputer.

Compilers And Interpreters.

All the higher level languages are finally translated into the machine language which is processed by the computer. The translation of higher level languages is accomplished by two kinds of software: **Compilers and Interpreters.** Compilers translate the complete program, written in a high-level language called a "source language" into the equivalent machine level program before the program is actually executed by the computer. An interpreter, on the other hand, translates each instructions separately as the computer needs it in order to process a given task. It means the interpreter must go back and forth from the program many a time for complete execution. In this process erroneous instructions are quickly detected and eliminated. However interpreters execute programs more slowly than those executed by compilers. Like assemblers, both compilers and interpreters are system software and, as such are typically obtained from computer equipment manufacturers.

Command Language.

Many programs, written to accomplish tasks contain keywords that make the programs perform certain functions. For example a simple program may include five commands: Search, Edit, Delete, Save and Merge etc. These are operation instructions which enable the users to learn and use software more easily. With these instructions, a user of the program can perform all of the functions of maintaining the user file. These instructions might be called the command language of the program.

Most modern computing systems of all types have an operating language which is contained within the program and which enables untrained users to perform system functions. Although the software itself is written in high-level language and is translated by a compiler into machine language, the user of the system never comes into contract with any of these levels of the software. The only instructions the user needs to know to perform the function of the system is the command language itself. In this sense one can refer the command languages as the highest level of software (J. Rice).

Command languages are also part of any sharing system, computer network, or online search service. These languages are developed carefully to be learned by users who have no knowledge of programming (J. Rice)

APPLICATION SOFTWARE

A computer application software is a user program. It is a set of instructions which tells the computer how to execute a specific task on the particular set of data provided. Application software for libraries contains a sequence of instructions designed to perform tasks such as preparing list of defaulters, list of outstanding book order, list of journals received and numerous other specific tasks done in library operation. Application software can be categorized in number of ways. These can be broadly presented as follow:

1. Organizational information processing (data processing and MIS)
2. Mathematical, statistical and modeling.
3. Information retrieval.
4. computer-assisted instructions.
5. Data Communication.
6. Process control.

The basic approach to develop and execute application software is very much similar for all types of computer application. The program is developed on a sequence of operations technically referred to as an algorithm. (Fig. 3.1 illustrates steps for programming.) An algorithm may be defined as a finite sequence of instructions to solve a problem. It is like a formula or recipe, in that its application will always produce an identical result if it is followed precisely. An algorithm is always developed by the programmer to solve a specific problem at hand and that in turn is used for developing a computer program. Much time is spent in inventing, refining and perfecting algorithms to solve specific problems. It is common to express an algorithm in the form of a flow chart, using boxes of various shapes to denote various functions. (Figure 3.2 is an example of a typical task oriented flowchart illustrating the algorithm.)

Fig 3.1 (Steps For Programming)

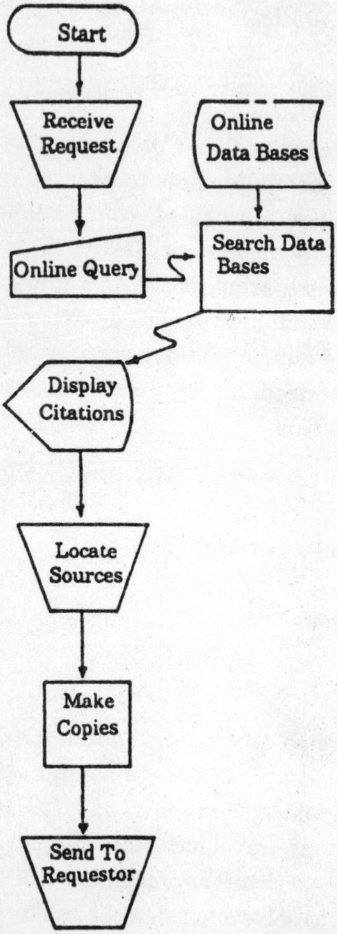

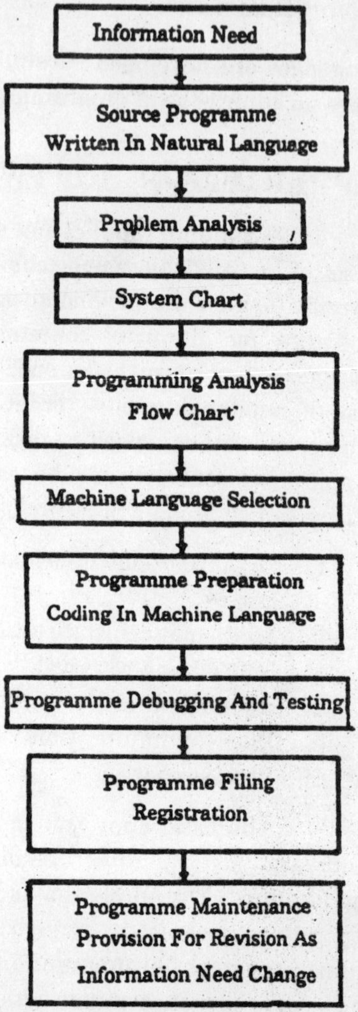

Fig 3.1 Steps For Programming

Fig. 3.2 Task Oriented Flowchart

As stated above developing application software is the user's responsibility. In general it is not supplied by the computer manufacturer. It is developed in-house or obtained from some other supplier. But writing in-house software is expensive and time-consuming. Instead the users prefer to purchase packaged or prewritten software. Some of the well-known packages developed as integrated library systems are discussed here briefly.

PACKAGED LIBRARY APPLICATION SOFTWARE.

DOBIS is a package for acquisitions, serials control and cataloguing developed jointly by IBM and the library at the University of Dortmund in West Germany. Leuven University Library in Belgium has produced a complementary package to DOBIS, known as LIBIS, to provide an online circulation facility. Examples of users of DOBIS/LIBIS include the National Library of Canada, Japanese Institute of Science and Technology, King Saud University, Saudi Arabia. DOBIS/LIBIS is used by over forty libraries in 15 countries. (Tedd).

NOTIS The Northwestern Online Total Integrated System (NOTIS) started to be developed in 1967 in US and is now in its third major version known as NOTIS III. It provides comprehensive online integrated processing capabilities for cataloguing, acquisition, serials control and circulation control.

Virginia Tech. Library System (VTLS) The library at Virginia Polytechnic Institute and State University has developed the VTLS system which integrates circulations, cataloguing records, serials control, acquisition, authority control and management reporting modules. The major design goals for VTLS were ease of use by library users and staff, good response time, visually pleasing displays and data access control. (Tedd).

Maggie's Place The Pikes Peak Library District in Colorado, US, has developed an integrated library system which is known as Maggie's Place. The basic functions supported include acquisitions, and processing, circulation, catalogue access, serials control and management. The community information file is also processed by the package.

The five longest turnkey (system) vendors are: CLSI, CTI, Library systems Inc., Data-Phase Systems, Geac Canada Ltd. and Universal Library Systems Ltd. The supply of application software, in these cases is a part and parcel of hardware.

Pak Book Library Package

In Pakistan Pak Book Corporation has developed a user-friendly software package (by using PCS Micro-Computers) to automatic library activities such as:

1. Inventory control.
2. Ordering and acquisition.
3. Cataloguing.
4. Circulation.
5. Serials control.
6. Information retrieval

It is a first standard software package developed by a Pakistani firm to operate outline. It may be preferred to in-house stand-alone system which is always expensive for small libraries.

The package has been developed under Foxbase Version 2.1 (Which is the fastest database manager available in the market). It has been designed to run on IBM or IBM compatible Computers-XT or AT with colour monitors (Screens) and DOS Operating Systems. However it can be used on monochrome (single colour) screens.

SOFTWARE DOCUMENTATION

Documentation is the set of materials which actually describe the purpose, operation, use and structure of computer programs. When a prewritten software is obtained, it is necessary for the purchaser to be well trained for ongoing software maintenance and use. Documentation therefore comprises detailed written information about the development of the software and the various aspects of the system. During the development of a computer program, documentation of how the program was designed is essential so that all people involved in a project will know what has been done and pass on this information to others. The system analysts and programers involved in a given software development effort are normally responsible for preparing appropriate documentation.

Davis and Rush, as quoted by Tedd, state that a complete software documentation package should include the following elements:

1. A statement of the problem to be solved.
2. A detailed description of the functions the software is to perform, and the functions that it permits the user to perform.
3. Definition of file structures to be used by the software.
4. Definition of the data structure to be used.
5. Definition of the data contents acceptable in these data structures.
6. Overall software design including algorithms to be used.
7. Computer system resources which the software will need for successful execution.
8. Other resources requirements (Personnel, equipment, materials).
9. Specification of the test data and procedures to be used to determine correct performance of the software once written.

After the programs have been written and tested:

1. Test results and software evaluation.
2. Execution cost estimates.
3. Detailed description of how the software works.

4. User manual.
5. Operations manual.

James Rice adds that the best documentation also includes self-teaching material (tutorials) to train users how to use the package. Because higher level languages are much closer to material language, it is understandable that their documentation would also be much easier to develop and much easier to understand.

Select Bibliography

Advances in Library and Information Science. v.1. Computer Applications. Edited by Dr. C.D. Sharma and Dr. D.C. Ojha. Jaipur RBSA Publishers, 1988.

Boehm, B. W., and Brown, J.R. Characteristics of Software Quality. New York: Elsevier, 1978.

Fosdick, Howard. Computer Basics for Librarians and Information Scientists. Arlington, Va: Information Resources Press, 1981.

Fundamentals of Computing. Edited by Graham Rowntree. Manchester: NCC Pub. 1987.

Libraries in the Age of Automation: a Reader for the Professional Librarian. New York: Knowledge Industry Pub., 1986.

Peterson, W.W. Introduction to Programming Languages. Englewood Cliffs, N.J. Prentice-Hall, 1974.

Rice James. Introduction to Library Automation. Littleton: Libraries Unlimited, 1984.

Spencer, Donald. D. Computers and Information Processing. Columbus: NCC Pub. 1987.

Tedd, Lucy A. An Introduction to Computer-based Library Systems. 2nd ed. New York: John Wiley, 1984.

Tucker, A. B. Programming Languages. New York: McGraw-Hill, 1977.

CHAPTER 4

Input / output Concepts And Devices

As discussed in the previous chapter, the primary storage or internal storage of a computer is located within its central processing unit (CPU). Sometimes this unit itself is called computer. This chapter elucidates the variety of devices which work with the CPU to produce a complete computing task. These input/out auxiliary or seconday storage devices are often called peripherals because they communicate with the computer from outside the CPU.

In the early day of computers, practically all input was done by using punched cards and punched paper tape. Even output was on punched cards or paper tape which was then fed into machines like telex printers or tabulator printers.

As computer systems have developed crossing their four generations from off-line batch processing through multi-access and time-sharing systems to online, real-time systems, so input and output devices have improved and developed a lot in parallel. Fig. 4.1 projects input/output devices.

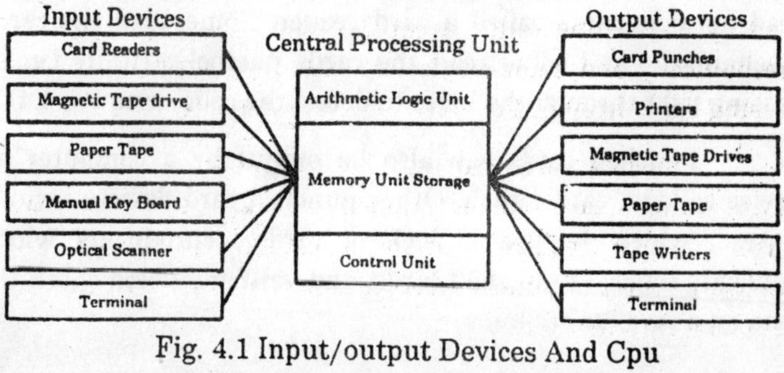

Fig. 4.1 Input/output Devices And Cpu

INPUT PERIPHERALS

The function of input peripherals is to convert human-readable information to machine-readable form required by the central processing unit. From amongst the available input peripherals, two types of equipment are commonly identified as being widely used. These are: Keyboard-oriented devices and optical recognition equipment. The Keyboard oriented devices feature a typewriter-like Keyboard on which the data are typed character by character (Fig. 4.2). On the other hand optical recognition also called electronic scanning uses reflected light to determine the content of material. Once identified, the data are encoded and recorded on magnetic media or transmitted directly to a computer Fig 4.3. Illustrates all methods of Input.

KEYBOARD INPUT

1. Punched cards

The first generation of keyboard-oriented input equipment recorded data in machine-readable form on paper media such as cards or tape generally identified as Punched cards and Punched Paper Tape. The Key-punch machine converts individually typed characters to a specified pattern of holes punched in successive columns of a specially designed card. A card is divided into rows and columns. Each column usually encodes one character which also appears in its usual readable form at the top of the card. The most widely used cards are 80 columns with row numbered 0-9. They can store eight characters of information per card. The cards are subsequently read by a machine called a card reader. Some read the cards mechanically and some read the cards photoelectrically i.e. by passing light through the holes to detect the code. (See Fig 4.4)

Punched cards can also be output by a computer on device called a card punch. Other punched card devices include sorters, which require a deck of cards; reproducers which duplicate copies of punched cards, and verifiers which check the data on a card for accuracy.

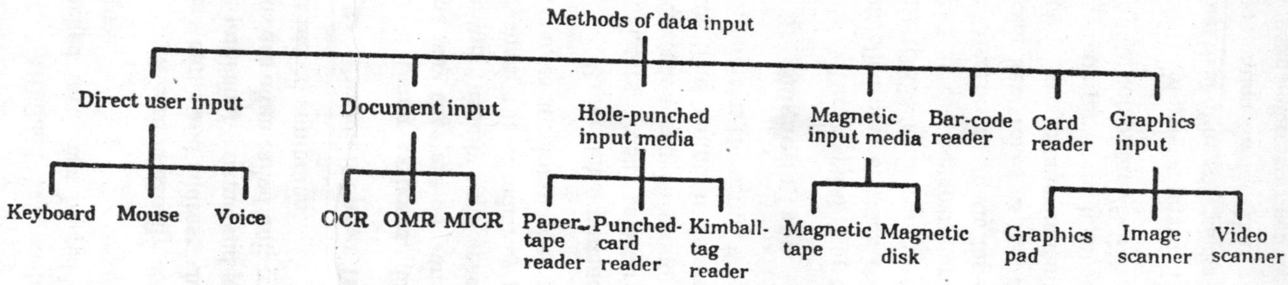

Fig. 4.3 The main methods of computer input

Fig. 4.2 A computer keyboard

Although keypunching cards is a slow process, the punched cards can be read at a rate of several thousand per minute.

A card is usually used to store a single record such as a user's name and address, the title and other data about a serial, or a publisher's name and address etc. Because of this, punched cards are often called unit records and their associated devices as unit record equipment.

2. Punched Paper Tape

Using keyboard, data are encoded on tape much the same way they are on punched cards. The tape is divided into columns (usually eight space wide) which run along the width. Information is encoded by punching the appropriate pattern of holes in each column. (See Fig 4.5)

Paper tape punches can be attached to typewriters, calculators, cash registers and other equipment so that information can be economically stored in computer-readable form. The computer record can therefore be produced at the same time as the actual typed document. (J.Rice). (See Fig 4.6)

3. Magnetic Tape

The typical key-to-tape unit is a microprocessor-controlled device which consists of a Keyboard, a cathode-ray-tube (CRT) screen and a magnetic tape recorder. Character typed at the keyboard are displayed on the CRT screen and recorded on magnetic tape. The keyboard being electronic can accept keystrokes as fast as the operator can enter them. The typical key-to-tape machine produces a reel or cassette of magnetic tape which must then be taken to a tape reader for input to computer. (See Fig 4.7-8)

Magnetic tape is inexpensive and durable and stores a great deal of heavily packed information. The computer can read tape much faster than it an read cards: several hundred thousand character per second.

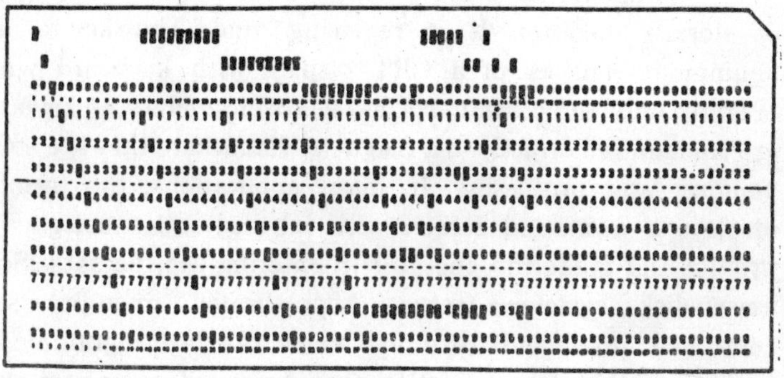

Fig. 4.4 Punched card

Fig. 4.5 Punched paper tape

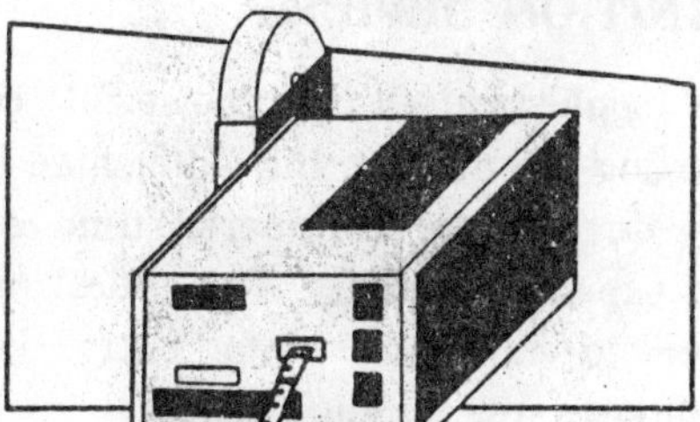

Fig. 4.6 Paper tape punch

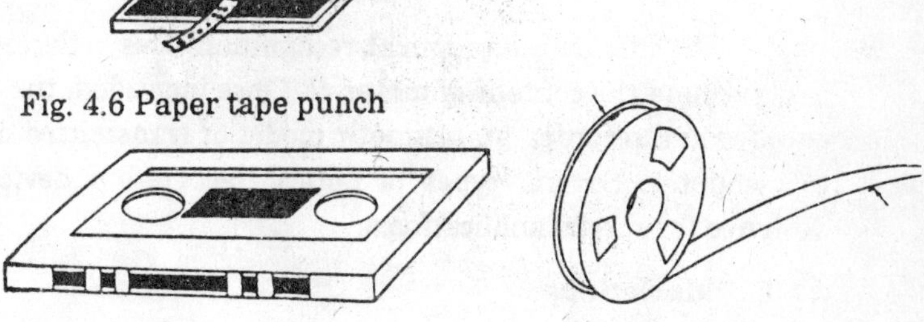

Fig. 4.7-8 Magnetic tape cassette and reel

4. Magnetic Disks

Magnetic disks are probably most commonly used type of storage medium. It is replacing tape. The key-to disk equipment consists of a CRT display with keyboard which operates online to computer. Characters entered at the keyboard are transmitted directly to a magnetic disk where they are stored pending later processing. In many applications, the terminal displays a formatted screen with labelled areas designed to prompt and guide the operator in entering specific data. Some key-to-disk systems feature sophisticated microprocessor-controlled "intelligent" terminal which can be programmed to perform certain data validation procedures before transmission. (Saffady).

Disks have several advantages over other media. Thousands of characters can be stored on each disk and the access time is extremely fast. Information can be input at a rate of about 200,000 characters per second.

OPTICAL RECOGNITION DEVICES

Since more sophisticated and powerful computing equipment are occupying the market, the old-fashion keyboard-oriented data entry devices are considered time-consuming, labour-intensive and expensive activity. The optical recognition technology attempts to minimize data entry labour by substituting electronic scanning for keystroking.

Broadly defined, optical recognition uses reflected light to determine the content of material. Once identified, the data is encoded and recorded on magnetic media or transmitted directly to computer. Several types of optical recognition devices are designed for special applications.

1. Mark-Sense

Mark-sense recognition relies on a specially designed input document with predesigned spaces to be filled in by pencil. Completed documents are then scanned by a machine which determines the meaning of individual marks by their location.

This device is widely used in educational application involving standardized multiple-choice examination. (Saffady).

2. Bar Coding

Bar code recognition is well known in libraries and retail stores. This device uses a specially designed label consisting of closely spaced lines of varying width to encode a number identifier. The label may be affixed to a document or other object and is scanned by a pencil shaped wand or a laser. The bar-coded label recognition device is used in library circulation systems.

3. Optical Character Recognition (OCR)

OCR is another type of optical recognition technology. It uses reflected light to identify the individual character content of input documents-letters, numbers, punctuation marks or special symbols. Since character vary in size and shape, each will reflect light differently. An input device called and OCR reader scans the material and identifies individual characters by comparing their light reflectance properties with definitions already stored in the computer. The identified characters are then encoded in machine-readable computer-processible form. Keystroking labour is eliminated.

OCR although looks attractive, has not been very successful due to the high cost of character recognition equipment.

4. Image Digitizer

While OCR readers accept textual documents as input a special type of optical recognition device called an image digitizer is designed to convert photographs, drawings and other graphic documents to machine-readable computer-processible forms. An image digitizer divides input documents into a series of rectangular picture elements, or pixels, each of which is analysed and its tonal value encoded. At present, image digitizers are not used for library application. (Saffady).

A final input technique which is still in its infancy, is speech input systems. The problems of machine recognition of human speech have proved difficult but some input devices do exist. Generally the machine is taught to recognize individual words spoken and will then be able to recognize and generate the appropriate codes for the word when spoken by that speaker. (Tedd).

OUTPUT PERIPHERALS

The function of output peripherals is to convert machine-readable, computer-processed data to human readable form. All output devices present the results of computer processing to users. A variety of output devices is available but not all of them are useful in library application. Instead, library automation relies only on those output peripherals which print information onto paper, record it on microfilm, or display it on a screen.

Although "Paperless" information is now available on large scale, paper printers still remain a very important type of computer output device. Even these computer systems which are heavily oriented towards screen displays use paper output for backup.

PRINTERS

Quite a number of printers are available in the market. They vary considerably in technology, output characteristics, operating speed and intended application. One could choose a particular printer depending on the office needs. The common types of printers available are categorized as follow:-

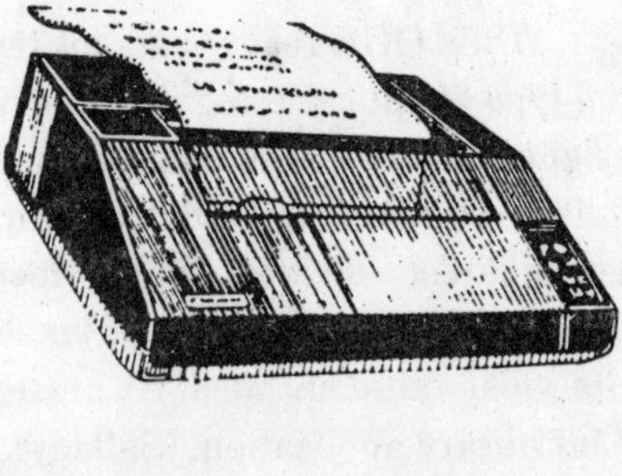

Fig 4.9 (A Printer)

1. **Impact Printers**
   i. Line printer
   ii. Dot matrix printer
   iii. Daisy wheel printer
2. **Non-Impact Printer**
   i. Ink-jet printer
   ii. Laser printer

Impact printers have been around for a number of years. They print by striking the type against the ribbon and paper (similar to a simple typewriter). Printers that can print only one character at a time are called "character printers" as against the "line printers" which print an entire line at a time. They can produce carbon copies, if necessary.

Non-impact printers are practically noiseless and create images only one at a time. They require special paper and provide better quality output than impact printers.

Line Printers

Line printer which prints an entire line at a time rather than a character is the fastest printer. Its speed varies from 300 to 3,000 lines per minute. It has been used in data processing applications for many years. They normally have 132 print positions per line.

Line printers generally produce only upper case (capital) letters though some provide both upper and lower case letters. The quality of printing is poor in terms of style and density for office use. However, they are used for internal reports in big organizations.

Dot Matrix Printer

Dot matrix printer is an impact printer which prints one character at a time. The print head comprises a matrix of tiny needles, usually seven rows and five columns. These are electrical driven and punch characters in the form of patterns of tiny dots. The pattern of dots for each character is dictated by the information held electronically in the printer.

Dot matrix printers can produce capital as well as lower case letters. Some printers have a capability of producing compressed or expanded letters. Its speed varies in the range from 40 to 600 characters per second. The printing is poor for business letters. Nevertheless, they are used extensively in word processing for internal correspondence and rough drafts. Matrix printers are much cheaper than the line printers.

Daisy Wheel Printers

Daisy wheel printer is a character printer and derives it name from the shape of the print wheel. The daisy shaped wheel is made of metal or plastic and holds characters on its petals. The wheel rotates at high speed and when the required character is positioned over the ribbon, a tiny hammer strikes it against the ribbon thus transferring the character symbol to the paper.

Daisy wheels are interchangeable and therefore different sizes and shapes of letters can be used. These are slow printers. The speed ranges from 17 to 200 characters per second. These produce good quality printing and are extensively used in word processing applications.

Ink-jet Printers

These printers print characters by spraying electrically charged ink onto the paper. These are capable of producing a variety of character shapes and sizes. The speed is around 100 characters per second.

Laser Printers

These are high speed, high quality printers. A laser beam is used to burn character images onto a rotating drum and the heated surface area picks up toner which is then offset to paper. Laser printers can produce around 15,000 characters per second. Though these can produce good quality characters of different styles and sizes and print even logos for letter heads, but are very expensive and are therefore not popular with small organizations.

COMPUTER OUTPUT MICROFILM (COM)

COM is a variant form of nonimpact output technology in which data is recorded on microfilm rather than printed onto paper. Actually, a computer output microfilmer, or COM recorder, is both a computer peripheral device and a high-speed microfilmer capable of recording document images at rates ranging from slightly less than 10,000 to more than 40,000 lines per minute. COM recorders are expensive.

Two recording methods are widely used: (1) in CRT photography, information displayed on a cathode ray tube contained with the recorder is microfilmed by a specially designed camera; and (2) in laser beam recording a laser writes alphanumeric character on thermally sensitive microfilm. With either method, document images are recorded in greatly reduced size on rolls of 16 or 35 mm microfilm or on sheets of 105 x 148 microfiche. The computer produces an index to locate the proper role and frame for a given output.

COM is often employed to create a back-up medium or to store historical data from a computer system.

SCREEN DISPLAY (TERMINALS)

Third category of output peripherals displays the result of computer processed data on a screen. These screen-oriented output devices are collectively called video display units (VDUs) and they are most often built with a keyboard to enable the VDUs to operate as interactive computer terminals. The basic functions of any terminal are those of data entry, data display and data communication.

Fig. 4.10 CRT

Terminals are basically of two types- printer terminals or video display units (VDUs), although one terminal may include both print and display, facilities. A printer terminal consists of a keyboard and a printer on which are recorded both the characters typed by the user and the characters transmitted by the computer.

The second type of terminal i.e. VDU consists of a television-like screen, which is used to display characters, and a keyboard. Most VDUs display 24 lines each of 80 characters, although some can now have 132 characters in a line. VDUs normally display information using a technique known as raster scanning, from a cathode Ray Tube (CRT). (See Fig 4.10)

AUXILIARY STORAGE MEDIA AND DEVICES

Auxiliary or secondary storage devices are designed to retain information in machine-readable form while awaiting computer processing. They supplement the necessarily limited capacity of the CPU's primary or main memory which is reserved for the storage of programs and the data that the computer is processing at a given moment. Earlier computer systems used paper media such as punched cards or punched tape for recording and storing machine-readable data, but now magnetic storage devices have become the most widely used means of auxiliary storage.

There are two types of auxiliary storage: sequential and direct access. Sequential storage is non-addressable, i.e. one cannot directly refer to he contents of a particular storage location. Using sequential auxiliary storage such as magnetic tape or cassette tape, entails going through the tape in sequence to locate the desired information. It is a searching by starting at the beginning and searching through all data records until the desired information is found. Direct storage also called random storage, allows users immediate access to information. Magnetic disks, floppy disks, wincheseter disks, magnetic drum, and video disks are all forms of direct access storage.

Magnetic Tape

Magnetic tape is a principal input/output device which provides a rapid way of entering data and recording processed data. Information is recorded on magnetic tape as magnetized spots called bits. The recording can be retained indefinitely or the information can be erased automatically and the tape reused many times.

As used in full sized and minicomputers systems, the typical magnetic tape measures one-half inch wide by 2400 feet long and is wound on a plastic reel. Regardless of its housing the tape is divided across its width into seven or more commonly, nine parallel tracks, each track being intended for the recording of one bit. The accumulation of six or eight parallel bits encodes a single character. Data are grouped in clusters called a logical record. Each record is physically separated from the next by a blank space called an interrecord gap (IRG).

The magnetic tape drive is the mechanism that pulls the magnetic tape into position past the read/write head. The read/write head converts the magnetized bits it senses on the tape into electrical pulses and transmits them to the central processing unit. When data are being written onto the tape, the read/write head magnetizes the appropriate areas and simultaneously erases any information previously stored in that location.

Magnetic tape is widely used as auxiliary storage. Upto 640,000 numerical characters per second can be read from or written onto a tape. While tape drives operate online i.e. connected to computer, the tapes themselves are typically stored offline. It is widely used in library application for the sale or exchange of bibliographic data. Magnetic tape is not a suitable storage medium for interactive and computing application in which data must be accessed rapidly and in more or less random order with respect to its recorded sequence. Such applications must use the more expensive direct access storage devices.

Magnetic Disk

Magnetic disk is used in full-sized minicomputer system. The typical magnetic disk is rigid, magnetic coated platter on which data is stored character by character in a series of concentric tracks, and is divided into a number of storage sectors. The surface is used to hold magnetised information that is written on and retrieved from the disk by a disk drive. In most cases two or more disks are aligned into a common spindle in a configuration called a disk pack. The capacity of disk packs varies with the number of platters and the density of recording at the present time ranges from 10 million to over 300 million characters.

Disks have several advantages over some other media. Their storage capacity, speed of access, reusability and ability to be in direct communication with the computer merit preference to tape media.

Although records stored on magnetic disks are often sequentially organized and processed like tape records, the popularity of disk storage is largely due to their direct access capabilities.

Floppy Disk

Floppy disks also called diskettes and flexible disks are popular media for auxiliary storage. They are widely used in microcomputer minicomputer, data entry, and word processing systems, as well as in remote terminals. The floppy disk is a compact flexible, magneticoxide-coated mylar disk. They are individually contained in envelopes or jackets for protection. It comes in three popular diameters: 20 cm, 13 cm, 9 cm. The last two are called mini-floppy and micro-floppy disk respectively. (See Fig 4.11)

Fig 4.11 (Floppy disk)

Information is recorded in digital fashion on the disk's magnetic surface which it is rotating. Entire disk is inserted into disk drive for reading or writing. Almost all micros now make use of floppies as the main secondary storage medium. They are comparatively inexpensive compact and easy to use.

Winchester Disk

Quite recently introduced winchester disk uses thin-film technology that permits bit densities of 12000 per inch. Winchester disks are sealed modules that contain both a disk and a read/write head mechanism. The sealed conditions provides protection against contamination, crash and losing data. For these reasons they are extremely reliable, and provide highest storage capacity.

Magnetic Drums

A less frequently employed form of direct-access storage is magnetic drum. It functions in much the same manner as disks. Data is recorded in tracks on magnetic-coated cylinder which rotates to position a specified sector of a given track under a read/write head. Although operate at somewhat faster reading and writing speed, they offer less storage capacity and are somewhat more expensive.

OPTICAL STORAGE

Optical disks and video disks represent an important and rapidly growing technology. Both the CD-ROM (computer disk/read only memory) or simply known as the "compact disk" and video disk are types of optical storage made possible by laser optics. VIDEO DISKS can store both pictures and text in extremely high density and provide fast access to individual frames on a disk. The visual images such as pictures, graphics, charts or print can be retrieved in motion picture form (for a movie) or still pictures, and can be retrieved in slow motion or reverse. A video disk is about the size of a long-playing record and can hold several hours of television pictures and sound or the equivalence of more than 50,000 photographic slides.

The use of videodisks with the computer system is still in the early development stage. One drawback is that videodisks only have play-back capacity; they cannot have data written on them. Therefore most applications involve entertainment and the storage of information is not dynamic in nature.

An **OPTICAL DISK** is next of kin to a videodisk. Binary digits are stored on this medium optically (using laser light) rather than magnetically. Optical disks store information with much higher density than magnetic disks do, and they provide extremely rapid access. Nearly all optical disks now in use are in a form of read only memory device. This means it cannot be re-recorded (like videodisk) over an over like magnetic media. However, the recent advant of erasable disk has solved this problem. (J. Rice).

One advantage of the optical disk is that plastic material used in the disk is not expensive. Optical storage is also now being packaged in other forms besides disks. These include cartridges and cards.

CD-ROM is designed specifically for machine-readable, computer processible data. Its main feature is that it is a permanent form of storage and the data recorded cannot be altered. It is being used as a means of distributing large amounts of information in a compact form. With 550 megabytes of data CD-ROM is useful medium for database publishing. The majority of CD-ROM publications produced to date are reference and research data bases designed for the library market where they offer a potentially cost effective alternative or supplement to equivalent databases offered by online search services on a timeshearing basis. One CD-ROM can accommodate complete Encyclopaedia Britannica. CD-ROM can also replace computer-output microfilm in certain types of micropublishing applications. The disks are read by relatively inexpensive drives (Saffady).

A typical CD-ROM can store about 300,000 book pages. The collection of Library of Congress Prints and Photographic Reading Room are on Videodisks, each of which holds about 54,000 separate pictures. (W.A.Katz).

Still another variety of compact disk is called COMPACT DISK-INTERACTIVE (CD-1). It is similar to CD-ROM, but has the advantage of storing not only text, but video and audio as well on a single medium.

HOLOGRAPHIC STORAGE

Recently a new form of storage device using laser technology to store information on holographic film is seen. Three-dimensional images can be stored and then read by light-sensitive electronic equipment. This enables binary information to be stored optically yielding an extremely high capacity and yet very rapid access. (J. Rice)

Mass Storage Devices

Where very large (multibillion or trillion character) data storage capacity is required, several available mass storage systems employ magnetic-coated tubes or strips stored in specially designed data cells. These data cells provide a kind of online tertiary storage for information which is used relatively infrequently and would otherwise have to be removed offline, or "archived" to magnetic tape (Saffady). An example of such a device is the IBM Mass Storage System.

Select Bibliography

Balagurusamy, E. Office Automation and Word Processing. New Delhi: Tata McGraw-Hill, 1987.

Changing Information Concepts and Technologies; a Reader for the Professional Librarian. New York: Knowledge Industry Pub. 1982.

Flowers, Stephen. Success in Information Processing. Suffolk: John Murray, 1988.

Fundamentals of Computing. Edited by Graham Rowntree. Manchester: NCC Pub. 1987.

Kent, A. Information Analysis and Retrieval. New York: Becher and Hages, 1971.

Kent, Allen & Galvin, Thomas J. (ed.) Information Technology: Critical Choice for Library Decision-Makers. New York: Marcel Dekker, 1982.

Rajaraman, V. Fundamentals of Computers. New Delhi: Prentice-Hall of India, 1985.

Rice James, Introduction to Library Automation. Littleton: Libraries Unlimited, 1984.

Rorvig, Mark E. Microcomputers and Libraries: A Guide to Technology Products and Applications. New York: Knowledge Industry Pub. 1981.

Spencer, Donald. D. Computers and Information Processing. Columbus: Charles E. Merrill Pub. 1985.

CHAPTER 5

Automation In Libraries

DEFINITION

Since the advent of the term automation in 1936, plethora of definitions are found in library literature. Sometime the terms 'mechanization and automation' looked overlapped, although there is a difference of one degree between the two. Mechanization was aimed at handling problems of bulk, weight and distance at replacing muscle and movement with machines. Automation is the name given to an automatic system of working. A few meaningful definitions are examined hereunder.

Encyclopedia Britannica Defines Automation

"The name given to an automatic system of working. The difference between automation and mechanization, a related term, is being mainly one of degree".

Mr. Harder introduced automation in 1936. He defined it initially as "the automatic handling of parts between progressive production processes".

Since then the term has been applied to a wide variety of automatic machinery and automatic systems, and is commonly used to describe any operation in which there has been a substantial substitution of controlled action for human efforts or intelligence.

Encyclopaedia Of Library And Information Science

Library automation is the use of automatic and semiautomatic data processing machines to perform such traditional library activities as acquisitions, cataloging, and circulation. Although these activities are not necessarily performed in traditional ways, the activities themselves are those traditionally associated with libraries; library automation may thus be distinguished from related fields such as information retrieval, automatic indexing and abstracting, and automatic textual analysis.

Linguistic purists have argued rightly that the term "automation" applies more correctly and narrowly to automatic process control, and indeed this was historically the first use of the term. The broader meaning, however, has had the sanction of widespread usage for a number of years, and "library automation" is now by far the most commonly used term for mechanization of library activities using data processing equipment.

GENERAL CHARACTERISTICS

The characteristics of an automated system are:

1. The operations/processes are carried out automatically.
2. Avoids or reduces human action and thus saves labour.
3. It accelerates efficiency and speed in operation.

HISTORY AND DEVELOPMENT OF AUTOMATION

From centuries together libraries have sought technological aid to facilitate and augment their service to readers. For example the introduction of a simple typewriter into libraries dates back to the late 1800s. Historically the phrase "Library automation" too has been used many a time synonymously with "Library Mechanization" which from some quarter was not considered quite accurate. On the other hand it was felt convenient to simply equate library automation with "computerization". But today without any controversy the term 'Library automation' is used extensively to refer primarily to the use of computers to perform some of the traditional library activities such as acquisition, cataloguing, circulation, and serial control etc. Conventionally the related fields such as information storage and retrieval (ISR) automatic indexing and abstracting, automatic text analysis etc. did not fall within the purview of 'Library automation'. This distinction has now almost disappeared. Information systems, is included in the context of automation. Although computers are playing primary roles in library automation today, the roles played by telecommunication technology, video technology, micrography, and reprography are of great significance because of the magnitude of support they offer to library automation.

Punched Cards Systems

Before the advent of computers, International Business Machines (IBM) and Remington Rand led the way to business technology by introducing equipment such as keypunch machines and electromechanical card sorters and collators. Although these devices were not computers, they had certain similar qualities such as they could read, compute, and manipulate data recorded in reusable form. William Saffady mentioned that as early as the 1930s and extending into the 1960s, a number of libraries in the United States had used punched cards in combination with sorters, collators, and other equipment as an alternative to manual record keeping.

In the United States Ralph Parker installed a Hollerith punched-card system for circulation control at the University of Texas in 1936 and by the middle 1940s had also experimented with its use in serial record control. In 1942 the Montclair Public Library of Montclair, New Jersey, installed "two specially designed book charging machines" which recorded individual transactions automatically in punched cards. The Library of Congress produced a book catalog using punched cards in 1950, and the King Country (Washington) Public Library another one in 1951.

These were scattered instances of mechanized systems, however. More were installed in the late 1950s and early 1960s, but most of these were in small, specialized libraries. Typically, such systems used standard punched-card equipment, sometimes called "unit record" equipment because the punched card as a unit record was central to its operation.

Computerized Library Systems

Computers were not used before about 1961, and in this respect library automation lagged behind business, industry, and science. The lag was not due to lack of interest and enthusiasm on the part of librarians, however; computers were still assumed by most people to be satisfactory only for numerical work, and computer programs were still oriented business and scientific applications. Even unit record equipment was difficult for most libraries to obtain until their parent institutions-universities, local governments, and businesses-had obtained computers.

The general purpose computers that were widely available in the 1960s opened new era of library automation systems. Punched card equipment remained in use, but played only secondary and insignificant role. Most of the computer systems common in the 1960s used punched cards for input and thus the information was fed into the system in a way like unit record systems. But once the data were entered many other operation could be performed during a single processing. More important aspect was that the system could "remember", storing information regarding book orders in progress, books held or on loan, periodicals received and so forth all on magnetic tape. Moreover, the information could be transferred automatically in and out of the computer "core" storage as needed for complete operations.

Availability of computers on wider scale, subsequent improvement in data processing capability, and reduced cost together gave impetus to growth and rapid development of library automation in the 1960s. Another realization that computer could be used effectively for non-numerical work further augmented interest in computer use.

While the 1960s saw the emergence of computer applications in libraries and the 1970s ushered in the online era, it has only been in the 1980s that automation has become a feasibility rather than a goal for the future for large number of libraries in the world. It makes the first half of the 1980s quite different from the previous decades but the later half added new dimension providing unimaginable facilities through variety of automated methods used for library operations.

NEED FOR AUTOMATION

Various factors have contributed to bring about change from conventional to automated library operation. Broadly speaking the main reasons behind this change are as under:

1. Growth Of Document

The amazing growth of documents especially in areas of sciences, social sciences and technology in the form of book and non-book material forced the library planners to utilize new technology for the organization of information since the traditional library methods failed to cope with the task.

2. Users Services

Heavy influx of documents added new dimension to user's needs. It is only the computers which can ensure improved and quick service. For example the manual work of housekeeping such as acquisition, cataloguing, circulation, serials control, etc. can be done with greater speed and efficiency with no arrear and backlog kept pending. Automated cataloguing provides variety of access points to a greater volume of information. Online catalogue has made it possible for a reader to press the key of the typewriter like terminal and have access to large bibliographical databases and obtain information in whatever field. It can be viewed on screen and if it is needed a printout can also be obtained. Mode·n services such as current awareness service and selective dissemination of information can also be introduced efficiently.

3. Greater Efficiency

The workflow in the library may be made more rapid, more systematic and efficient with the help of the computer. The records in the computerized store are more accurate, more reliable and more accessible than the manually prepared records. All sorts of housekeeping jobs and information works can be performed with more speed, accuracy and greater efficiency.

4. Cooperation And Resource-sharing

No single institution, however resourceful can now collect, organize all documents available all over the world even in a specific field. Nor any one organization can collect all documents in the areas of interdisciplinary and multidisciplinary subjects. During the last two decades there has been an increase in cooperation and resource-sharing on the part of libraries by developing computer-based systems. It has two advantages: (a) access to more documents and information sources due to coordination and cooperation of many libraries in a system and (b) less expenditure, because the total cost is shared by a number of library in the system. The computer-based library systems, such as Online Computer-based library centre (OCLC) in the United States, the University of Toronto Library Automation System (UTLAS) in Canada and the Birmingham Libraries Cooperative Mechanization Project (BLCMP) in the U.K. are functioning successfully with increasing databases and multidimensional services.

The advantages of library automation are far-reaching. Housekeeping jobs aside, the facilities of time-sharing and online services have made library automation more effective for efficient and appropriate service. Today only computerized library can take part in computer networking and information networks at national and international levels. It is the only way in which efficient standardised and faster service is assured, besides access to a world of information and data.

COMPUTER APPLICATIONS IN LIBRARIES

The application of the computer to library operation has two aspects namely housekeeping routines and information storage and retrieval. The housekeeping routines include acquisition and ordering work, cataloguing, circulation control, serial control, and keeping of records, statistics for overall management purpose. The application of computer to information service comprises generation and collection of information, information retrieval, current awareness services, selective dissemination of information, computerized databases, information transfer and distribution etc.

In the field of housekeeping routines, the job description amenable to computerization in each area is outlined as follows:

1. Acquisition Work

(i) Selection of material
(ii) Checking of duplication
(iii) Ordering work
(iv) Preparation of order cards/slips
(v) Sending orders (offline or online) to suppliers/vendors
(vi) Updating record file
(vii) Verification of books with order file and invoices
(viii) Accession work
(ix) Print out of received and non-supplied documents
(x) Control of book budget i.e. expenditure incurred and balance.

2. Cataloguing

(i) Preparation of Authority file/thesaurus or subject Heading list
(ii) Original cataloguing (offline or online)
(iii) Arrangement of catalogue cards into classified, alphabetical or subjectwise alphabetical.
(iv) Preparation of shelf-list

(v) Preparation of list of catalogued item (accession list) in any desirable form.

(vi) Provision of access points in a variety of ways and in an appropriate physical form.

(vii) Centralized/cooperative and shared cataloguing possible.

3. Circulation Control

(i) Registration of members

(ii) Issuance of borrower cards

(iii) Charging and discharging of items

(iv) Preparation of overdue and recall notices

(v) Updating of record file

(vi) Managing of book reservation system

(vii) Calculation of necessary fines for overdue books

(viii) Detection of problem borrower at the point of issue.

(ix) Maintaining statistics in variety of forms.

4. Serial Control

(i) Selecting suitable title for purchase

(ii) Generating purchase orders; renewal and new

(iii) Receiving issues and claiming issues not received

(iv) Preparing catalogues of serials and other records.

(v) Keeping current and accurate details of serials holdings.

(vi) Allowing access to details of current holdings.

(vii) Routeing individual issues to various members.

(viii) Organizing completed volumes of serials for binding.

(ix) Exercising budget control and producing management information.

In the area of information retrieval process three tasks are generally performed by the computer, i.e. indexing, storage or organization of information in a desired format, and retrieval or recall of information whenever required. Job description amenable to computerization is outline as under:

Information Retrieval Process

(i) Indexing of documents
(ii) Preparation of Thesaurus
(iii) Abstracting
(iv) Inter-library loan
(v) Reproduction of documents
(vi) Compilation of Union Catalogue
(vii) Bibliographic work
(viii) Searching and providing printouts of relevant information

In order to meet demand of the user, libraries have to build up their own databases with the help of computers. Catalogues, indexes, bibliographies, union catalogues are, in a sense example of databases. They only need conversion into machine-readable form. These jobs are now widely done in libraries. Databases on specific subjects, interdisciplinary and multidisciplinary areas are also being created in the library for anticipated and potential use of the patrons. The kinds of databases prepared in the library are usually known as in-house databases. But their creation, organization, arrangement, storage, retrieval and distribution is entirely based on automation.

Libraries too have access to external databases. These databases are created, promoted, and maintained by local organization, national and international agencies to provide access to comprehensive information resources on specific areas for their own research and need. Some scientific and technical organizations also establish databases and make them available to customers on commercial basis. The only condition for the libraries to have access to the external databases is that they must have a compatible computer system, be prepared to process software packages or be connected by online facility within the country or outside the country.

The databases may be divided broadly into four groups according to their purposes and contents, viz, bibliographic databases, non-bibliographic databases, textual/numeric bases, and catalogue record databases. The bibliographic databases such as INSPEC, SCISEARCH, COMPENDEX, CHEMABS, MEDLAR, BIOSIS hold comprehensive data on science, science citation index, engineering index, chemical abstracts, medicine, biological sciences respectively. There are many other such computerised bibliographic databases. The non-bibliographic databases are of the directory type. They hold actual text or information rather than references in machine-readable form. They mostly concern with business, financial statistics, industrial data, social sciences, economics, banking, marketing etc. Librarians are closely concerned with these databases. Such databases are accessible via the similar channels as bibliographic databases. Textual/numeric databases are also non-bibliographic and include numeric, textual-numeric, properties and full text databases. The catalogue record databases are online computerised catalogues of national libraries like the Library of Congress, National Library of Canada etc. These are all machine-readable catalogues (MARC). If, a library has a set of compatible computer, the MARC tapes can be used in great variety of purposes. For example printed catalogue for public use can be obtained out of the MARC tape mechanically.

In the United States and Europe, computer is heavily used for current awareness service. The users are kept informed of the latest information in their respective field. Selective dissemination of information (SDI) has been computerized in number of libraries. The service comprises two kinds of jobs: description of documents received and preparation of users profiles indicating their areas of interest. Computer easily does matching function and transmits information with the least human involvement.

Thus the use of computer in various library activities has proved Landau's concept of 'Library-in-a disk' a reality. This revolutionary concept which envisages 'Paperless Information System' or according to Lancaster 'Paperless Society' has brought about drastic changes in library outlook. As stated before, in developed countries manual library operations are fast vanishing giving way to automated systems. These modern and dynamic innovations are providing library service as "Libraries without walls" with an ability of free access (or paid) to world information. But the role of librarian has not diminished in this changed scenario; it is being modified to make him an Information Specialist.

Select Bibliography

Adams, Roy, J. Information Technology and Libraries: a Future for Academic Libraries. London: Croom Helm, 1966.

Becker, J. and Hayes R.M. Information Storage and Retrieval. New York: John Wiley, 1968.

Encyclopaedia Britannica. Chicago: Encyclopaedia Britannica, Inc. v. 2, 1966.

Encyclopaedia of Library and Information Science. v. 14, New York: Marcel Dekker, 1968.

Kent, Allen. Information Analysis and Retrieval. New York: Wiley Becker, 1971.

Lancester, F.W. Toward Paperless Information System. New York: Academic Press, 1978.

Libraries in the Age of Automation: a Reader for the Professional Librarian. New York: Knowledge Industry, 1986.

Mahapatra, Piyushkanti. The Computer in Library Service. Calcutta: The World Press, 1985.

Muhammad Riaz. Documentation and Information Work. Lahore: Qadiriyya Books, 1989.

Rice, James. Introduction to Library Automation. Littleton: Libraries Unlimited, 1984.

Rowley, Jennifer F. Computers for Libraries. London: Clive Bingley, 1985.

Saffady, William. Introduction to Automation for Librarians. 2nd ed. Chicago: ALA, 1989.

Tedd, Lucy A. An Introduction to Computer-based Library System. 2nd ed. New York: John Wiley, 1984.

Telecommunications and Libraries: a Primer for Libraries and Information Managers. New York: Knowledge Industry, 1981.

CHAPTER 6

Automated Circulation Control Systems

Circulation of books and other materials is an important part of library public services. This section deals very delicately with the reader's community. Here one finds flow of reading materials, but the flow must be controlled by library operation so as to serve the users in the best possible way with the available resources. It is the duty of this section to check misuse and promote proper use of library documents. Simultaneously, it is necessary to record the movement of material, maintain statistics in order to display strength and weakness of stock and provide guidance for collection development in future.

It is also expected that circulation should be as simple, speedy and effective as possible. All the stage of movement must be recorded and records cumulated. The books requested for reservation must be trapped and the user served.

The objectives of circulation control may be summarised as follows:

1. To get information about the books to be borrowed, whether they are in the library or not.
2. To identify the borrower by particulars, such as name, address, borrower number, category, whether membership is lapsed, present status, borrower's signature, etc.
3. To identify the document to be borrowed, such as call number, ISBN, other identification number, author, title, edition, year etc.

4. To record the borrowing with particulars, such as the date of loan, the date of return, to whom it is loaned, any restriction regarding the loan, category of the loan, etc.
5. To ensure rapid charging and discharging of documents.
6. To trap the reserved documents.
7. To keep records of the number of books on loan to individuals.
8. To check overdue books and to prepare reminders.
9. To update loan files.
10. To prepare statistics.

THE DEVELOPMENT OF AUTOMATED CIRCULATION

Circulation control is one of the most widely automated library operation, and it is often the first activity that libraries consider automating. There are several reasons for this. For example most circulation control operations are clerical in nature. Their routine is error-prone in filing and related record keeping activities. Charging and discharging of library materials with an annual circulation of over 200,000 is highly labour-intensive. In most cases accurate maintenance of circulation statistics is impossible.

Saffady has pointed out that as early as the 1930s and extending into the 1960s a number of libraries in the United States used punched cards in combination with sortors, collators, and other "Unit record" equipment as an alternative to manual record keeping. Such "precomputer" data processing systems were typically based on inventory control models used in business. But in the mid-1960, with the introduction of computers for business applications, a number of libraries developed computerized circulation control systems based on offline (batch-processing) technique.

BASIC SYSTEMS

A computer-based circulation control system should perform the following functions:

1. Provision of information on the location of circulating items- either all items or only those items on loan or elsewhere, i.e. at the bindery, on reserve, being recatalogued, etc.
2. Identification of items on loan to a particular borrower or class of borrowers (namely, off-campus users).
3. Recording of *holds* or *personal reserves* for items on loan but desired by another borrower, often with additional provision for notifying the library staff when the item is returned and printing a *book available notice* for mailing to the person who requested the item.
4. Printing recall notices for items on long-term loan.
5. Renewal of loans.
6. Notification to the library staff of overdue items and printing of overdue notices.
7. Notification to the library staff or problem borrowers (i.e. those with unpaid fines, or overdue books) either at the time of an attempted loan, or at the time a borrower is leaving the institution or on request from the library.
8. Calculation of fines, printing of fine notices, recording receipt of fines, and sometimes printing of fine receipts.
9. Calculation and printing of statistics of various types.
10. Analysis of both summary statistics and statistics for the circulation of particular items for use in acquisitions, planning of services and for other administrative purposes.
11. Provision for handling special categories of borrowers and special types of materials, and

12. Provision for printing due date slips, automatically generating orders for lost books or needed (additional) copies and printing mailing labels for remote borrowers.

These functions may not be considered necessary for all libraries. The outline just elucidates the possible features of an automated circulation control.

FILE

1. Main File

Main file is the main component of circulation control. It records all loans and contains the record of each book not available in the library stock. Every record contains at least the minimum information, such as the book number, the borrower number and the date of borrowing. The main file is the loan file. If bibliographic information is not included in the loan file, another file called the book file is maintained.

2. Borrower File

In addition to main file, a borrower file is also maintained on magnetic tape. It includes one record for each authorized borrower. Like the manual card file each borrower's record consists of such fields as identification number, name, address, telephone, privilege category, registration date, and expiration date. The identification number may be a random number with alphabetical digital character or it may be structured number with certain information about the borrower. Coded information in the borrower number allows analysis of the use made of the library or to impose limit on the number of books to be loaned and the loan period etc. On the tape, borrower records are usually arranged in identification number order.

3. Document File

Some libraries maintain document file which contains information about Document Identification Number (DIN), author, title, edition (if any) volume, year of publication, name of publishers, and place of publication etc.

The Document identification number (DIN) can be anyone of the following:

(1) Call number, (2) Accession number, (3) Alphabetic random code, (4) ISBN and copy number, (5) Random number, (6) Any other locally structured number.

TRANSACTION AT CIRCULATION DESK (OFFLINE)

At the charging desk, the input is made to the computer. It relates primarily the book number and the borrower number. Both are assigned and identified uniquely. In the offline computer, the input is made in the batch processing system and in the online computer, it is made in the random access processing system. In the batch processing system, the data capture device transmit data to the paper tape or the magnetic tape cassette or floppy disc at the issue desk and then processed periodically. The computer may hold a trapping store to indicate reserved or problem borrowers. Trapping-store system consists of some electronic store which is capable of holding a document identification number (DIN). When the book is returned, the DIN is checked against the numbers held in the trapping-store. If the number is present, then a lamp glows which indicates that the document is reserved.

If the offline computer is used and no device for trapping the reserved books is attached to it, the computer printouts with the previous input of such lists that may be used as check lists. In case more than one copy is available in the library for a book requested for reservation, the book numbers may be linked to catch the book borrowed or information of other copies obtained from the main file. The computer can check the dates of returns of the books and thus prepare reminders for overdue books. These can be produced by line-printers. In the offline computer, over-borrowing can be checked after the due date is over. The updated transaction records prepare printouts with borrowers numbers. Updating of loan files from time to time prepares the corresponding records also from time to time. The statistical records can be kept on the basis of the transactions.

Although batch-processing circulation systems can eliminate the maintenance of paper file and time-consuming preparation of overdue and recall notices associated with manual system, there exists a gap in time between the action (counter transaction) and the computer's processing and reporting of information. The result is that some of the information contained in batch-processed lists become outdated. Also in batch processing circulation systems "hold" function for reservation of book is not automatic. A separate card file or list is maintained manually and consulted for each item reserved etc.

On-line System

In an on-line system the details of transactions are entered through a terminal connected to a computer directly. One can obtain up-to-the-minute information through the terminal. But, the main problem with mot of the libraries is the lack of continuous on-line facility even with parent authority's computer.

Hybrid Approach

Tedd reveals that some circulation systems whilst being predominantly batch do allow online access to the files of items on loan, etc., but such a file would only be accurate as of the last time it was updated. This mixture of batch and online processing is sometimes referred to as 'hybrid'. The majority of currently available systems, especially the turnkey systems, are online and real-time; this means that as soon as an item is issued or returned the relevant files are instantly updated and the most current information is immediately available.

DATA-CAPTURE DEVICES

The data capture devices are used in the library, either offline or online, to record transcription of books and the borrower on the pre-printed form. Then these data are converted to the machine-readable form and made input to the computer.

1. VDU Terminals

The recent innovation is visual display unit terminals or tele-typewriter terminals. In this case, self-adhesive labels with sensitive bar codes are required for each book. The data capture terminal 'read' the book card and the borrower card and 'write' data as required.

2. Label Based Systems

The Automated library system (ALS) UK has developed a label based system. This system is based on cards. The book number and the borrower number are punched on two cards. Both the cards are placed in a reader at the time of borrowing, and the information is transferred to the paper tape. The ALS system has also a label based device. In this device, a non-magnetic metallic label is placed on the book. The label has metallic dots. At the time of borrowing, the borrower card having a similar label is passed over the sensing device with the book label. Thus, the data is written on some machine-readable medium.

3. Light Pen System

The 'Plessey' developed a light pen system in 1972. It is a device for the graphical input and consists of a photo detector mounted on a pen-shaped holder. As the pen is held over the displayed element, it senses the light created on the patterns of the bars printed on the self-adhesive label, while the electron beams projected on them are picked up and sent to the computer as signals. As the computer knows the elements of signals, the data is written in the computer. The label with bar is transformed into the digital number. (See Fig 6.1). Every book in the library is assigned a given label with a unique number of identification, and a similar label with the borrower number having unique identification is held on the identification card of the borrower. The light pen method eliminates all cumbersome procedures of keeping the hand copy record or input media. No book card is required because identification is made

Fig. 6.1 (A light pen)

by the unique label. By holding the light pen on the book label and on the borrower label, the transaction is made within seconds, the fastest job in circulation control. The Plessey light pen system is a widely used device. The book and the borrower numbers are encoded on labels as thick and thin bar or line code. The light-sensitive pen does the job quickly. (Mahapatra)

6416249 2 UDC
BAILEY FWJ/FUNDS OF ENG
METALLURGY & MATERIALS

Specimen of Bar Coded Book Label

510004

EXPIRES 07.78

SIGNATURE

Specimen of Bar Coded Borrowers' Card

Fig 6.2 Bar coded labels for books and borrowers.

4. Stored Programme Control System

Another device is the Telepen consisting of the teletypewriter and the light pen. Both alphabetic and digital characters are encoded on labels. It incorporates a minicomputer that can be linked to a mainframe. It can also record transactions independently on the magnetic tape. It may also be equipped with a trapping store. The Stored Programme Control (SPC) is a hybrid system which provides added facilities. The system has a minicomputer to act as and enlarged trapping store and it is also connected with a large computer for processing data on the magnetic tape.

In some automated systems where issuing and returning of items is not very high, the labelling of the stock is not necessary. It is also a problem that some labelling systems require special 'readers' in order to convert the data into the appropriate bits for input to the computer system. Other systems require special sensing devices. For example, as mentioned before, bar-coded labels are usually 'read' using light-pens which includes a light sensitive device which can be used to decode the pattern of thick and thin lines in the bar code. OCR labels are usually 'read' by a hand-held OCR wand.

DEVELOPMENT FROM 1970s TO DATE

Batch-processing circulation systems reflected the situation prevailing in the 1960s and early 1970s. Through the mid-1970s, most automated circulation control systems were customed-developed for a single library or library system. As stated before, in batch processing keypunch or key-to-tape devices were used to convert information about individual circulation transactions to computer-processible form. The resulting data were then batched for processing at predetermined intervals etc.

By the mid-1970s, library automation specialists had begun to concentrate on the development of online, real-time circulation control systems which process circulation transactions as they occur. Since data files are updated immediately, such real-time systems accurately reflect the status of a library's circulation collection. Printed lists are replaced by online terminal inquiries to determine the circulation status of specific items.

While real-time circulation control system are custom-developed (inhouse) for individual libraries, some vendors in U.S. offer generalized preformulated approaches to automated circulation control that eliminate the need for customized system. Such preformulated approaches, according to Saffady, fall into two groups: (1) prewritten circulation control software meant for execution on a computer system; and (2) turnkey systems, consisting of preconfigured combinations of hardware and software. It is marked as self-contained products.

The early (1970s) prewritten circulation control software packages and turnkey circulation systems were single purpose products. But later on the domain experts developed integrated, multifunctional turnkey systems and software packages which combines circulation control with other capabilities. In addition to circulation control, the most complete integrated system comprises application modules for cataloguing, online catalogue access by library users and/or staff, acquisitions, and serials control, a community bulletin board system, and electronic message transmission.

Whether designed as single purpose products or as integrated systems components, prewritten circulation software packages and turnkey systems can be implemented for more quickly than customized circulation control systems which may require months or perhaps years to develop. Likewise prewritten software packages and turnkey systems minimize or eliminate requirements for local software expertise. Library using them don't need to hire programmers.

While prewritten circulation control software packages are available for computers of all types and sizes, libraries, medium-sized or large have typically relied on mainframe and minicomputer-based products. Examples of IBM mainframes include the NOTIS software package; IBM's own DOBIS/LIBIS program; and the TECHLIB/STATS implementation of the

BASIS software package. Minicomputer-based turnkey circulation control systems are available from CLSI, Geac, Data Research Associates (DRA), OCLC, Universal Library Systems and other vendors in U.S. (Saffady).

Select Bibliography

Automated Circulation: an examination of Choice. Edited by J. R. Mathews and Kevin Hegarty. Chicago: ALA, 1984.

Bahr, Alice Harrison. Automated Library Circulation Systems, 1979-1980. 2nd ed. White Plains, N.Y.: Knowledge Industry Publication, 1979.

Boss, Richard W. General Trends in Implementation of Automated Circulation Systems. *Journal of Library Automation* 12: 198-202.

Mahapatra Piyushkanti, Dr. The Computer in Library Service. Calcutta: The World Press, 1985.

Matthews, J. R. Choosing an Automated Library System; A Planning Guide. Chicago: American Library Association, 1980.

Rice James. Introduction to Library Automation. Littleton: Libraries Unlimited, 1984.

Rockman, Ilene. The Potential of On-Line Circulation Systems as Public Catalogues: An Introduction. *RQ* 20: 39-58. (Fall 1980).

Simpson, George A. Automated Circulation Systems in Public Libraries. McLean, Va. The Mitre Corp., 1978.

Swihart, S. J. and Hefley, B.F. Computer Systems in the Library. Los Angeles: Melville Pub; 1973.

Tedd, Lucy A. An Introduction to Computer-based Library Systems. 2nd ed. New York: John Wiley, 1984.

CHAPTER 7

Automated Cataloguing

As with the computerized circulation control, the Librarians have been interested in automating cataloguing systems. Unit Record Equipment were the first used as mechanized methods for cataloguing purpose in 1940s. The catalogue data were Keypunched and the punched cards were filed in relevant sequences. Many punched-card catalogues were produced and printed in 1950s. Saffady reports that precomputer equipment such as card sorters and paper-tape typewriters were in use in 1940s in United States. The computers were first applied in early 1960s to produce catalogue cards and book catalogue. Hence typewriters became redundant around mid 1960s.

It is obvious that during 1960s computers were used in cataloguing but in batch processing system. In batch processing, catalogue data were punched in cards and then transformed in the paper tape or magnetic tape. In some machine, however data were directly input in the punched paper tape or recorded on the magnetic tape. Gradually, programmings were made on the magnetic tape or discs which could be manipulated automatically. But in this period different libraries used different types of computers and there was no uniformity in the catalogue card format. The individual libraries had to spend a large sum on the custom-developed computer system in order to attain speed in work. This situation warranted the necessity for standardization of catalogue data and shared cataloguing. Thus the two aspects of cataloguing system developed during 1960s, became the most vital for computerized cataloguing. These are the standardization of the catalogue entry with the standard bibliographic description having a unique identification mark for each document with the International Standard Book Number (ISBN) and shared cataloguing under a computerized library system using MARC format. Different ISBDs have been prepared by IFLA to attain uniformity through computer.

AUTOMATED CATALOGUING SYSTEM

Automated cataloguing is possible by adopting any one of the following systems.

1. Participating in a bibliographic utilities, such as OCLC, WLN, etc.
2. Using commercially available systems such as Mini or Micro MARC or software package used primarily for cataloguing.
3. Applying integrated system which is also used for acquisition and or circulation purpose.
4. Utilizing book jobber or COM vendor services.
5. Adopting simple local input from the acquisition system.

What Is MARC ?

MARC is an acronym derived from Machine-Readable Cataloguing. Within the United States, the terms MARC, LC MARC and USMARC are interchangeable. The term do have slightly different meanings such as follow:

1. MARC is a generic term applied to the universe of MARC formats, including UKMARC, CANMARC, InterMARC, and so on;
2. LC MARC refers to the set of options and content designation called "MARC II";
3. USMARC is a new name of LC MARC, introduced in the Underlying Principles document in 1983. There is no

sharp distinction in content between LC MARC and USMARC. The term USMARC or MARC are also applied to MARC extensions, formats such as OCLC MARC and RLIN MARC that include data in addition to USMARC data.

MARC I

MARC I pilot project began in April, 1966 in which sixteen libraries participated. By the year 1968, the Library of Congress had distributed over fifty thousand English language monographs records. The purpose of MARC I was the automation of cataloguing, indexing, searching and retrieval functions. The participating libraries made better use of the MARC tapes distributed by L.C., in a variety of ways in producing catalogue cards, book form of union catalogues, specialized lists of materials under subjects, lists for acquisition on purposes and the like. The LC MARC database-the accumulation of Library of Congress cataloguing data in machine-readable form-now contains more than 2.5 million records.

MARC II

The MARC I format was based entirely on the structure of the L.C. catalogue cards and covered monographs only. Encouraged by the success of MARC I, staff of the L.C. started redesigning the procedures and programmes to cover material in other forms, and developed character set to include all the major Roman alphabet language as well as. Romanized forms. Meanwhile the British National Bibliography (BNB) showed interest in the UK MARC Pilot Project. Similarly interest was also shown by many foreign libraries to design a standard communication format suitable for interchanging bibliographic data not only from one source organization, the L.C., to many participating libraries, but also for exchanging information on cooperative basis among libraries at the international level. The US, the UK and other countries wanted a machine-readable catalogue format that would be a common one for international exchange of cataloguing and bibliographic data. Such an interchangeable record format was designed and was called MARC II.

It was a one-format structure on the machine-readable medium capable of containing bibliographic data of all forms of library materials, such as books, monographs, serials, maps, music etc., and related records. The structure or the physical representation of the machine-readable medium; the content designators, such as tags, indicators, and subfields codes used to identify the data elements; and the content or the data itself such as author, title and bibliographic descriptions are the three components of the LC MARC format.

MARC II officially began in March, 1968. Distribution began for all English Language material providing a weekly magnetic tape of zonal 1000 records. Thereafter, other documentation begain to be issued, including formats for other materials over the period 1970-73. In 1972 films records were distributed, by 1973 records for serials, maps and French books, by 1975 German Spanish and Portuguese materials.

MARC II is a subscription service. By subscribing to this service a library can acquire, in machine readable form cataloguing data for American and other foreign publications as described above. In fact the Library of Congress catalogues the documents i.e. books and non-book materials, records the data on magnetic tape and supplies copies of the tapes to various interested libraries. The libraries which get the copy of magnetic tape, can then produce printed catalogues of their collections entries on cards and various kinds of bibliographies (author or subject etc.) by using a computer. Most libraries obtain access to MARC data through products and services developed by publishers computer system developers, time-sharing services and other intermediaries. MARCFICHE is the earliest of MARC-derivate products. At present a growing number of vendor supply the MARC database on CD-ROM disks or digital optical videodiscs accompanied by software which supports the retrieval of specific cataloguing records and the printing of card sets. Example include the BIBLIOFILE.

Uses Of MARC

MARC tapes are being used for various purposes. Following are some of their important uses:-

1. A centrally prepared catalogue can be distributed to the receiving libraries in a machine-readable form.
2. In spite of increasing acquisitions, the catalogue can be kept up-to-date without employing additional staff.
3. The production cost of card catalogue on the computer (MARC System) is lesser than that of purchasing the Library of Congress catalogue cards.
4. The MARC tapes can be utilized for acquisition functions i.e. selecting, ordering and claiming unsupplied books without any additional cost. They can be used to produced spine labels, book pockets etc.
5. The MARC tapes can be used for producing conventional card catalogue by the subscribing libraries, as demonstrated by the University of Toronto.
6. The MARC data can also be used for producing book catalogues as demonstrated by the Washington State Library.
7. The MARC tapes can be used for computerised SDI service.
8. It automatically performs resource-sharing functions.

Mini or Microcomputer-based MARC is commercially based cataloguing system. Practically a microcomputer is housed in the Library and a set of floppy disks is provided which contains the entire MARC database. It is then quickly retrieved and edited as needed. (J. Rice).

LIMITATIONS

George Piternick points out the following few limitations of the Machine-Readable catalogue systems:

1. The MARC record for any title is almost similar to the conventional bibliographic record, as such it inherits all its limitations.
2. The MARC format will be limited, at least for the next few years, to the English language books because the MARC character set is severally limited in respect of special characters and diacritical marks.
3. The time gap between the creation of MARC record and a catalogue record copy by the participating library, which is inherent at present in the existing card production methods of the Library of Congress, will not be removed until and unless both the cards and tapes are prepared from the same machine-readable record.
4. Expenditure on account of machine time by the participating libraries will go on increasing in view of the weekly shipment of about 1,200 records or about 62,000 records annually requiring 15,000 feet of magnetic tape.

MARC records are no longer created only by L.C. but also by many other agencies, and are available through bibliographic utilities and from commercial services.

Retrospective Conversion (RECON) In MARC

The MARC Distribution Service was enlarged and proved to be efficient in making conversion of all current intake into the machine-readable catalogue. But all these were for the current holdings of libraries only. Librarians were interested to the preparation of machine-readable catalogue of their older holdings and to replace their card catalogues with machine-readable catalogues. But it was realized that uncoordinated activities by individual libraries would entail expensive repetition of work in converting the existing catalogue into the machine-readable form. Personalised efforts would also be devoid of uniformity in headings and forms.

RECON Pilot Project was initiated in August 1969. It continued for two years and approximately 58000 records were converted. The most significant technical achievement of this project was the development and implementation of the format recognition process.

The British Library is also converting to machine-readable form all records printed in the British National Bibliography and they include all books published in Britain since 1950. The retrospective catalogue conversion made by the British Library is held in the BNB/LASER file which keeps more than 700,000 MARC records from 1950 onwards.

UNI MARC

The implementation of US MARC, UK MARC and ISBD, the increasing number of national MARC formats etc. created an environment for international cooperation in interchanging bibliographic data. The IFLA Working group discussed some of the problems encountered in the area of universal standardization and agreement on content designators in machine-readable format. The concept of SUPER MARC as an international system for exchange of information was agreed upon in principle.

A draft of the international MARC format was made in 1975 for universal use. Finally, for international exchange of MARC records, a new machine-readable format was designed and is known as UNI MARC. It has been envisaged that the national organizations producing MARC records will produce them in the national standards for use within the country and will reformat them according to the UNI MARC format for international exchange. The international and universal MARC has become a reality.

ONLINE CATALOGUES

The growth and development of MARC for machine-readable cataloguing of current materials and the retrospective conversion of manual catalogues to computerised ones represent the history of the offline computer system in library cataloguing. The process of creating and editing the records in the batch system through the offline computer was however labour-intensive and time-consuming. The capabilities of the online computer system for random access and operation in "real time was realized by the library administrators. The libraries planned to use the online system for cataloguing. During the early 1970s, the online system was used in its early phase. In the online system, the machine-readable files, either MARC or local were transferred from the magnetic tape to the magnetic disc or drum where random access was possible. Visual display units (VDU) or computer terminals were used for input and output operations, and these terminals were fitted with the line printers for the hardcopy output.

Defining The Online Catalogue

What exactly constitutes an online catalogue is difficult to explain satisfactorily. A few important definitions are recorded hereunder. Library of Congress defined it as follows:

> "An online catalogue is an access tool and resource guide to the collections of a library or libraries, which contains interrelated sets of bibliographic data in machine-readable form and which can be searched interactively on a terminal by users".

National Library of Medicine gave a compact definition:

> "[An online catalogue provides] online access to the complete bibliographic record of all the library's holdings with minimal access points being the same as these available in a card catalogue".

Research Library Group (US) gave a characterized definition of online catalogue as follows:

An online Catalogue:

1. Provides the public with direct access to a library's bibliographic data base through the use of a terminal.

2. Is searchable through a variety of access points greater than those available through card form catalogue.

3. Is searchable with a common command language which may be transferred when the public moves from one library to another.

4. Retrieves information from a local library file, and if not successful locally, retrieves information from other libraries files.

5. Provides instructional help.

6. Displays such results in readily understandable form.

7. Provides links to card form catalogues, reference help, circulation files, etc.

8. May be accessed remote from the Library's location.

These definitions were written in 1980, but as of 1983, there was still little consensus as to what an online catalogue really is. James Rice attempts to feature online catalogue as under:

"An online catalogue is a fully interactive catalogue of holdings that has the potential of being accessible in any number of ways. It is by far the most dynamic form of catalogue because the user does not need to adapt to any physical limitations (e.g., dictionary listing, divided catalogue, or book pages). Users simply input a query. such as an author's name, subject headings, or keyword from the title, and the computer responds with an answer that allows for further communications".

In sum, an online catalogue is an organized, machine-readable accumulation of bibliographic records which are maintained on disks or other direct-access computer storage media for retrieval by library users and staff members working at interactive terminals or appropriately configured microcomputer workstations. In addition to saving space and automating file maintenance, online catalogue permit remote access by authorized persons equipped with compatible terminals, and they can support information retrieval operations such as keyword searching of titles and series names. (Saffady).

Online catalogue may be custom-developed (inhouse) for specific library use or purchased as prewritten software packages or turnkey systems. Examples of custom-developed online catalogues include the L.C. computerized catalogue, the MELVYL system at the University of California, the Library Computer System (LCS) at Ohio State University. Prewritten software packages suitable for online catalogue implementations include BRS/SEARCH from BRS Information Technologies, a powerful information retrieval program that is available in mainframe, minicomputer, and microcomputer versions. Besides this several vendors in U.S. and elsewhere offer turnkey information storage and retrieval systems which include preconfigured combinations of hardware and software components suitable for online catalogue implementations, STAR system is an example.

Since the mid 1980s online catalogue practice has been dominated by integrated library systems which combine database management and catalogue access capabilities with circulation control, acquisitions, serial control, and other operations. Such systems may be implemented as complete turnkey systems or as prewritten software packages designed to operate on a library-owned mainframe, minicomputer, or microcomputer.

Most recently for online catalogue implementation, large number of vendors in U.S. offer public access catalogue systems which employ CD-ROM storage technology. Examples include the IMPACT system from Autographics, THE INTELLIGENT CATALOG from the Library Corporation, and the LEPAC system from Brodart. In such implementations the library provides a machine-readable version of its catalogue typically consisting of MARC format records on magnetic tapes obtained from bibliographic utilities or other sources, to a CD-ROM system vendor who indexes and otherwise prepares it for conversion to one or more CD-ROM disks. CD-ROM catalogues are now increasingly mentioned as an alternative to COM for union catalogues and similar implementations.

BIBLIOGRAPHIC UTILITIES

Most libraries in the United States, Canada and elsewhere, instead of developing their own inhouse systems prefer to obtain access to machine-readable cataloguing record through one of the bibliographic utilities, i.e. organizations which maintain large databases of cataloguing records and offer online access and other services to subscribing libraries only. Examples include the Online Union Catalog implemented by the Online Computer Library Center (OCLC), the Research Libraries Information Group (RLG), the cataloguing support service operated by the Western Library Network (WLN), the Cataloguing Support System (CATSS) offered by Utlas International, Canada, the LIONS system operated by the New York Public Library and so on. The British Library Automated Information Service (BLAISE) is also now one of the world's largest commercial services. Its catalogue production is made through LOCAS (Local Catalogue Service) which is an integral part of BLAISE.

While these organizations differ in database size and composition, the number and nature of their subscribers and the specific capabilities they support, each maintain a database of L.C. MARC records, supplemented by original MARC-format cataloguing contributed by subscribing libraries. Working at local terminals, participating libraries can retrieve cataloguing copy, modify it to meet local needs, and order printed card sets, machine-readable cataloguing records on magnetic tape, and other bibliographic products. Supporting thousands of online terminals, accessing millions of machine-readable records, the

Bibliographic Utilities are among the world's largest and most intensively utilized computer-based information services.

Online Cataloguing With Bibliographic Utilities

Any library which is a member of centrally located database like OCLC or RLIN etc., is given facility for online processing of cataloguing records. By having access to a central database, an individual library can make use of the existing records in the most efficient and effective manner for a number of purposes. Following is a brief review of some of the key processes involved in online cataloguing.

Terminal

On-line cataloguing is performed on a terminal installed in member library. This terminal is connected to a central database subscribed by the Library.

The terminal generally consists of two parts-a CRT (cathoderay tube) terminal, which looks like a television receiver, and an attached keyboard similar to that of a typewriter except that it contains special functions keys for system use and special library characters. Many terminals are accompanied by line printers.

Searching

The main purpose of searching is to ascertain whether a particular record is in the database.

Searching is generally performed by means of search keys. The search keys may consists of alphabetic characters, numeric characters, or both. The most commonly-used search keys are derived from the following elements in a record: name-title, name, title, subject entry, LC card number, ISBN, ISSN, and a special control number in the data base.

Frequently, a particular search key may call up more than one record, because the computer will respond with all the records containing the same search key. In such a case, a list of the items containing only brief information will be displayed and the searcher then decides which particular record in the list is to be displayed in full.

If the inhouse terminal reports that the record for the item in hand is already in the data base, it can then be used for any purpose. From cataloguing standpoint, the cataloguer compares the item being catalogued with the record held in data base. If there is no variation, the record then can be processed for cataloguing purposes i.e., card can be printed from the record; and the record can be added to the library's own tape for producing COM catalogues if required. However if the record varies in certain details from the item being catalogued, it can be modified or edited to suit individual purposes. If the item in hand is not held in data base, the cataloguer on his terminal keyboard catalogues the item in accordance with the standardized entry format and then it is automatically added into the central data base.

One great advantage of on-line cataloguing is the instant feedback. In editing, the modification made to the information displayed on the screen, and the modified or edited record is shown instantly to ensure that all necessary modification have been correctly processed.

Inputting Cataloguing Records

The inputting process is used to store cataloguing data in machine-readable form in a data base. After the cataloguing information has been identified and organized according to cataloguing rules, the subject headings and call number have been assigned, and the individual elements have been encoded or tagged according to the MARC format, the record is then ready to be input into the computerized data base.

The inputting process can also be performed in an on-line mode through the terminal. Results of input can be displayed immediately for proof reading and any necessary correction.

COM

COM (Computer Output Microfilm) catalogue developed as an outgrowth of book catalogue. COM recorder is a type of nonimpact computer printer which converts machine-readable data to microfilm or microfiche without creating an intervening paper copy. The process begins by first converting the catalogue into machine-readable form. The database is then stored on magnetic tape or disk or some other secondary storage medium. The microform output is usually on 105 x 148 mm. microfiche or 16 mm. microfilm. The COM format is getting popularity. Special Readers are required for the magnified display of COM-generated images. Reader/printers can be used to create paper copies. In US and UK several book jobbers and vendors have developed software capable of producing COM catalogue from library supplied, machine-readable bibliographic data. It eliminates the need for an inhouse COM recorder. Also several of the bibliographic utilities themselves offer COM catalogues as an output alternative. Firms such as Brodart, Blackwell North America etc. are active in this market.

COM catalogues offer several advantages. Some are outlined hereunder:

1. It is inexpensive to reproduce and can be placed in many locations inside and outside of a library.
2. There can be separate films for author entries, title entries, and subject entries.
3. Several records can be viewed at one time.
4. Entries can be easily copied if a microform reader/printer is available.
5. Equipment is relatively inexpensive.

Some disadvantages of COM are

1. Microforms are often not very readable compared to print.
2. It is not easily updated.

3. Updating is by supplements which may confuse the catalogue user.

4. The microfiche format may lead to interfiling of a base catalogue with supplements.

5. Deleted materials remain in the file until the next update.

6. Special microform reader/printers are expensive.

As COM catalogues gained popularity in the United States and elsewhere, several vendors attempted to introduce special readers for library applications. These readers can store upto 1200 feet of 16 mm. microfilm-the equivalent to twelve ordinary rolls on an internal reel. In most cases, the library's on-line COM catalogue can be contained in this reel which remains inside the reader and need not be handled by the user.

OPAC

Library automation has finally introduced online public access catalogue (OPAC). James Rice reports that at present more than 50 libraries in the United States are using this form of catalogue. Although most of these are in large libraries, a few are in medium-sized or even small libraries. Many more libraries are also trying to adopt OPAC. Such catalogues allow any member of the library community to search the catalogue data base in order to see if the library holds specific title of document, to be informed of its location in the library, and if the catalogue system is linked to the circulation system, the enquirer be intimated whether the item is readily available or is on loan to other etc. It is stated that the availability of turnkey circulation systems have contributed to the development of OPACs and Geac turnkey system is getting much popularity in the libraries of UK and US.

IN-HOUSE AUTOMATED CATALOGUING

Library automated systems were first developed at local level in the United States. In fact some of the automated systems identified with vendors or bibliographic utilities were actually based on systems that first existed in individual libraries.Where in-house system is introduced, the libraries usually maintain a main file of catalogue records of the libraty's holdings. It is regularly updated and generally printed at periodic intervals. When in a library computerization starts, there is every need to convert retrospective catalogue into machine readable form and add it to the main file to make it complete.

Following are the main processes involved in a cataloguing systems:

1. Preparing worksheet.
2. Generating machine-readable records.
3. Verification of the records and generation of the catalogue.
4. Generation of added entries.
5. Generation of indexes and cross-reference.
6. Printing the records.

The output depends on the physical form of the catalogue chosen by the library. The chief forms are:

1. Line printer paper catalogue
2. Phototypeset catalogue
3. Microform, and
4. Card catalogue.

MARC FIELDS (ACCESS POINTS)

Before computer-based cataloguing starts, the library has to resolve many problems such as the actual and potential use of the library by the staff, students and other users; the length of data entry for various other usage within or without the institution etc.

Tedd referring to a research made at Bath University says that the following MARC fields can satisfy over 97 percent of readers requirements:

TAG DEFINITION

CONTROL FIELDS

001 Record Control number
050 LC call number
082 Dewey Decimal classification number

MAIN ENTRY HEADING FIELDS

100 Personal name main entry heading
110 Corporate name main entry heading
111 Conference, congress, meeting etc., name entry heading

TITLE FIELDS

240 Uniform-title - excluding collective-title
245 Title and statement of responsibility area.
248 Second level and subsequent level title and statement of responsibility.

EDITION FIELD

250 Edition area

IMPRINT FIELD

260 Publication, distribution, date, etc.

NOTES FIELD

503 Edition and history note

SUBJECT HEADING ETC. FIELDS

600 Personal name subject heading
610 Corporate name subject heading
611 Conference, congress, meeting etc. subject heading

ADDED ENTRY HEADING FIELDS

700 Personal name added entry heading
710 Corporate name added entry heading
711 Conference, congress, meetings, etc. name added entry heading
745 Title added entry heading-excluding uniform title
800 Series added entry (personal name-title)
840 Series added entry (title)

Automated Cataloguing Procedure

For designing in-house computerized cataloguing, the Librarian and the programmer should keep in view the length of information that could be expected from the catalogue. But it is not essential for local libraries in Pakistan to provide all the fields given in MARC record. The following fields can be sufficient in a medium-sized library:

1. Classification number
2. Main entry (personal or corporate)
3. Title
4. Imprint and collation
5. Series statement
6. Subject headings
7. Keyword entries
8. ISBN/ISSN/LC Card number

Coding Structure

To evolve coding structure for codifying the fields (type of entry) is technically a part of system designing. A logical coding is required for developing inhouse software which is based on: (1) Overall system designed (2) type of computer language to be used for development of computerized system. However in some latest computer free format, pattern comprising all the parameters, has been developed. Cataloguer can use and skip any field (access points) at one time depending upon the length of cataloguing data required without changing the entry codes every time.

Swihart and Hefley illustrate type of entry codes which is reproduced in the following table. This code identifies to the computer the type of data a record contains. (See Fig 6.3)

Type of Entry	Method 1 short Mnemonic	Method 2 Longer Mnemonic	Method 3 Numeric
Computer index number	CI	CINDEX	01
Security restriction code	SR	SECUR	02
Corporate agency author	CA	AUTC	12
Personal author	PA	AUTP	14
Title	TI	TITL	22
Report number	RN	REPNO	31
Contract number	CN	CONNO	33
Grant number	GN	GRANO	35
Number of pages	PA	PAGES	51
Number of illustrations	IL	ILLUS	52
Number of figures	FI	FIGS	53
Date of publication	DP	DAPUB	54
Place of publication	PP	PLPUB	55
Abstract	AB	ABSTR	61
Subject heading	SU	SUBJ	71
Keyword	KE	KEYWD	73

Fig. 7.1 Type-of-entry codes.

The above table is illustrative only. It is not applicable to any one library. If the practicing library is not using a standardized software, it can develop its own type-of-entry-code on such patterns.

DATA INPUT

Records may be entered 'off-line' or 'on-line'. With the off-line an input form is normally completed by the cataloguer which is then passed to a punch or other operator for 'translation' into a machine-readable form, e.g. punched cards for inputting to the computer. With the on-line, records are entered direct into the computer via an on-line terminal keyboard.

1. Computer Index Number

The computer index number is consecutive (accession) number which has no intrinsic value. This number is assigned to every title in the library.

2. Main Entry

It is established according to AACR2 or name authority file for oriental names etc. Cataloguer using name entry code, types the name of the author on the keyboard of the computer. It appears on the screen. If the name of the author already exists in computer held record, it is skipped. Traditionally the author entry has been considered the "main entry". But with a computer system, there is no main entry in that sense. Author or title entries have no more importance as such. All entries in automated system stand equal.

3. Title Entry

Titles are entered into the record in the exact format and spacing in which they should appear in the printed catalogue cards. Subtitle is entered in subfield. If software allows title can be permuted to offer more approaches to the important words in the title. Stop words are ignored.

4. Imprint and Collation

Imprint implies the place of publication, publisher and date. Publishers are entered under place, followed by publisher name. It follows title entry and then collation is recorded.

5. Series Entry

A name/title series entry is given if desired. Both name and title series are stored in name and title files respectively.

6. Subject Headings

L.C. or Sears' List of subject headings can be used for alphabetical subject access. Thesauri are used in specialized subject fields. Subject headings can be entered as required either in plain alphabetical language form or as a numerical subject entry code as are given in thesaurus etc. Subordinate subject headings can also be used if the system program allows.

7. Keyword Entries

Keyword entries can be provided by permuting titles. This increases access points and strengthens subject approach in the catalogue.

8. ISBN/ISSN and LC Cards Number

The ISBN/ISSN access point file contains International Standard Book Numbers and International Standard Serial Number that may be used as access points when searching cataloguing database. Pakistan ISBN serves the same purpose. They all provide unique identification of an item and are convenient search keys. The LC Card number APF contains LC card numbers assigned by the Library of Congress. They may be from LC MARC cataloguing record or from the item in hand.

ADVANTAGES OF AUTOMATED CATALOGUING

Innumerable benefits are accrued from automated cataloguing practice. There is no time-lag between accessioning and cataloguing. Routine and repetitive jobs are done efficiently. Besides the catalogues, a variety of records is produced as by-products. These are the catalogue cards or machine-readable records that serves as a basis for the production of COM or book catalogue, various printed records, book plates, book pockets, book cards, spine labels etc. It is also possible to use COM for the production of Union Catalogues, bibliographies, Reference tools. The computerized catalogue can be integrated into a total information system particularly in academic and special libraries. It encourages cooperative cataloguing and centralized cataloguing.

In the on-line system direct input can be made through the terminals. It is also possible to correct, revise or amend the data on the existing record format required for new editions of the same titles. The authority files can be kept. Sorting and filing sequences can be rearranged according to requirements.

Catalogue entries and catalogue data can be arranged by specified criteria and in various sequences, such as the number of books on a subject or by an author, list of books on a specific subject, list of books written by a particular author, list of authors on a particular subject, and the like.

Select Bibliography

Attig, John, "The Concept of a MARC Format" *Information Technology and Libraries* 2: 7-17 (March, 1983).

Crawford, Walt. MARC for Library Use. New York: Knowledge Industry Pub. 1984.

Epstein, H. The Technology of Library and Information Networks. *Journal of the American Society for Information Science* 31: 425-37 (Nov. 1980)

Fayen, Emily Gallup. The On-line Catalog: Improving Public Access to Library Materials. New York: Knowledge Industry Pub. 1983.

Friedman, E.S. "Patron Access to On-line cataloguing Systems: OCLC in the Public Service Environment". *Journal of Library Automation* 6: 132-39 (July, 1980).

Hostage, J. "AACR2, OCLC and the Card Catalog in the Medium-Sized Library". *Library Resources and Technical Services* 26: 12-20 (Jan.-March, 1982).

The Library and Information Manager's Guide to On-line Services, by Ryan E. Hoover and others. New York: Knowledge Industry Pub. 1980.

Mahapatra Piyushkanti, Dr. The Computer in Library Service. Calcutta: The World Press, 1985.

Malinconico, S. Michael and Fusana Paul J. The Future of the Catalog. New York: Knowledge Industry Pub. 1979.

Maruskin, A. F. OCLC: Its Governance, Function, Financing and Technology. New York: Marcel Dekker, 1980.

Matthews, J. R. "The Four On-Line Bibliographic Utilities: A Comparison". *Library Technology Reports* 15: 665-838 (Nov.-Dec., 1979).

Matthews, Joseph R. Public Access to Online Catalog: A Planning Guide for Managers. Weston, Conn.: Online, Inc., 1982.

Rice James. Introduction to Library Automation. Littleton: Libraries Unlimited, 1984.

Rockman, I.F. "Potential of Online Circulation Systems as Public Catalogs". *RQ* 20: 39-58 (Fall, 1980).

Saffady, William, "Library Automation: an Overview", *Library Trends* 37: 269-81 (Winter 1989).

Swihart, S. J. and Hefley, B. F. Computer Systems in the Library. Los Angeles: Melville Pub; 1973.

Tedd, Lucy A. An Introduction to Computer-based Library Systems. 2nd ed. New York: John Wiley, 1984.

CHAPTER 8

Automated Reference Service

From the very beginning reference service has been defined in variety of ways. Wyer defined reference service as "that part of library administration which deals with the assistance given to the readers in their use of the resources of the library". Margaret Hutchins narrates "reference service includes the direct aid within a library to persons in search of information for whatever purpose and also various other library activities especially aimed at making information as easily available as possible".

Broadly speaking the function of reference service is to assist library users in obtaining access to required information. It is entirely a public service activity in which the librarian functions as a professionally trained information specialist. Much of the reference work entails two types of transactions. Firstly it is a ready reference question which requires a factual response. Secondly, it is literature searching activity which demands more time to prepare bibliographies on specific topics.

Methodologies employed to answer both the queries are the same. The reference librarian interviews the enquirer to clarify the question; formulates strategy, and then appropriate sources are identified. In response, the enquirer is directed to these sources. In other words the librarian actually does the search and provides factual information or bibliographic citations to the enquirer.

Before 1940s all types of reference activities were manually operated, that is the preparation of bibliographies in specific topics relied on printed indexing and abstracting journals. Bibliographic listings and other sources providing access to monographs, periodical literature, technical reports etc., were manually prepared. In 1950 punched cards were used for data processing and information storage. These are the immediate predecessors of computer-based systems of 1960s.

Machine-Readable Reference Sources

For an automated reference service, the availability of machine-readable reference sources is an indispensable prerequisite. The early 1960s witnesses the era of offline computer-based systems. During this period (1960s-1970s) many publishers of printed bibliographies and indexes started using computer-based text-editing and photosetting techniques. Saffady states that in the late 1960s and early 1970s, publishers of indexing and abstracting journals and bibliographies began to sell machine-readable versions of their products in addition to or in place of their printed equivalents. This data was and is still offered on the reels of magnetic tape. MARC tapes are among the earliest examples of such machine-readable bibliographic data products. Today many printed indexing and abstracting journals and bibliographies are available in machine-readable versions and commonly used in computerized online information retrieval systems. These machine-readable products are sometimes called bibliographic data base.

DATABASE

The term data-base denotes an integrated accumulation of computer-processible data organized in a manner suited to a wide range of applications. It is synonym today for a collection of printed or numeric records which have been transformed and stored in a computer. A database may range everything from a standard index, to an encyclopaedia, to a statistical collection such as census reports etc.

Databases may be classified into the following categories:

1. Bibliographic (or Reference) databases
2. Non-bibliographic or (source) databases

Generally speaking, bibliographic databases are a series of linked bibliographic records, with each record containing some combination or permutation of the following components:

(a) document number
(b) title
(c) author
(d) source reference
(e) abstract
(f) full text
(g) indexing words or phrases
(h) citation, or number of references
(i) organization originating the document, or author's address, or both
(j) language of the document
(k) local information, e.g. location, special classification numbers.

These components constitute a document reference which contribute to bibliographic control by facilitating the retrieval of relevant documents when they are needed. Such a document reference does not normally give the information itself, but rather indicates documents in which information might be located.

Bibliographic databases may be created by local information units. In addition, there are larger, internationally accessible databases which can be searched with the aid of international telecommunications networks.

Most machine readable bibliographic databases have their origin to an abstracting or indexing journal. Some databases and their printed equivalents are:

Database	Printed Equivalent
MEDLARS (Medical Literature and Retrieval system).	Index Medicus
INSPEC (Information service in Physics, Electrotechnology, Computers and control)	Science Abstract
COMPENDEX (Computerized Engineering Index.)	Engineering Index
ERIC (Educational Resources Information Service).	Resources in Education
BIOSIS (Bioscience informtion service)	Biological Abstracts
SCISEARCH	Science Citation Index.

Some of the available machine-readable bibliographic databases are interdisciplinary in nature and can be considered general reference sources. For example LC MARC, UK MARC CANMARC which contain cataloguing records pertaining to published materials regardless of field. News and current affairs databases are also interdisciplinary scope. Examples include NATIONAL NEWSPAPER INDEX, NEWS SEARCH AND MAGAZINE INDEX, the NEWSPAPER INDEX. Other examples of interdisciplinary bibliographic database include:

1. Books in Print.
2. British Books in Print.
3. Comprehensive Dissertation Index.
4. Ulrich's International Periodicals Directory.
5. Monthly Catalog of U.S. Government Publication.
6. British Official Publications.

Data-bases dealing with a single scientific or technical discipline are more numerous. MEDLARS, BIOSIS PREVIEWS, CA SEARCH; INDEX CHEMICUS.

Some highly specialized scientific disciplines are served by a number of machine-readable bibliographic databases. Examples include AQUACULTURE, WATER RESOURCES ABSTRACTS, WATERNET. Field of Engineering is covered by two important databases such as COMPENDEX and INSPEC.

Broadly defined nonbibliographic database contains data other than citations to books, articles, or other library materials. Nonbibliographic database is further divided into two groups:

(1) Textual data bases which contain information equivalent to that found in printed reference sources as encyclopaedias, directories, and periodical publications; and (2) Numeric data bases or other quantitative information. Numeric databases consist of information expressed as numbers presented in the form of tables or time-series'. They usually comprise a measurement (population or quantity), a time-series (months, years etc.) and a variable (production, imports, exports etc. of a specific commodity).

Today the Academic American Encyclopaedia, the Encyclopaedia Britannia, Everyman's Encyclopaedia and many other are available as machine-readable data-base accessible through the online search services. The ACADEMIC AMERICAN ENCYCLOPAEDIA is also available in CD-ROM and videodisk format.

Directory type data-bases are among the most common nonbibliographic reference sources available in machine-readable form. ENCYCLOPAEDIA OF ASSOCIATIONS is an example. BIOGRAPHY MASTER INDEX is a mixed bibliographic and nonbibliographic data-base which serves as a master index to biographical information found in directories, dictionaries, and other published sources. The number of bibliographic and nonbibliographic databases is growing all the time. CD-ROM is being heavily used for this purpose alongwith other optical storage devices.

Multidisciplinary and specialized search services share a common operating methodology. The commercial organizations purchase or otherwise obtain bibliographic and nonbibliographic databases in machine- readable form from their producers; convert the databases to a desirable form for storage on their computers, and allow libraries or other subscribers to perform various retrieval operations on such data using prewritten databases management software. (Saffady).

ON-LINE INFORMATION RETRIEVAL SERVICE

During the late 1960s and early 1970 information retrieval service remained offline. After receiving query, reference librarian used to formulate suitable search strategy consisting of a combination of commands and search terms. These search requests were then key-punched and batched for processing against one or more data bases at predetermined schedule. When processed, the computer used to produce printed lists of citations for each request. The search results consisting of these retrieved citations (output) would be mailed to the enquirer or the originating library.

But from the mid 1970s the era of online information retrieval starts. In an online system, machine-readable bibliographic data base is maintained on disc for interactive searching by librarians working at local terminals. The computer terminal in the library is usually linked by telephone to a large mainframe computer in a city which may be 20 to 3000 or more miles away. In this mainframe computer is stored the needed information in a database. The Librarian or the searcher analyses query and formulates search strategy consisting of a commands and search terms. While interacting, he just enters the commands with the help of terminal keyboard and the result is seen on the video display unit or cathods ray tube. The print out is not possible by the VDU unless the matter is printed by the connecting printer. Here if the user needs a printed record of citations, he just pushes a button and the records are immediately printed out.

Online computer search is just like two way conversation between searcher and computer system. Therefore, online system is also referred to as interactive i.e., conversational or real time which means as they occur'. This interaction takes place through terminal connected to computer through communication lines. Thousands of abstracts and indexes, bibliographic and nonbibliographic data are stored on discs and used online.

Some government bodies and corporate libraries in the United States and Europe have developed their own online search capabilities, using machine-readable bibliographic data bases created locally or purchased from publishers of printed indexes and abstracting services. Most libraries, however, use the external online search services for retrieving details of published items on a particular subject whereas previously they have used printed abstracting and indexing journals.

A computer search is neither complicated nor difficult. Anyone can learn, although it takes time to be skilled searcher. Here comes the reference librarian who acts as intermediary because the average user has neither the skill nor the time to search.

Essential Components

Computerized online information retrieval systems have now taken several forms and have numerous components. According to Katz the basic delivery system for online service consists of:

1. Hardware which is usually a terminal connected via telephone lines to a mainframe large computer.
2. Software or instruction to computer which makes it possible to effectively and quickly search for specific bits of information.
3. Databases which are the electronic equivalent of the printed reference works and are searched by a computer. These are available from vendors and/or publishers, some are fee-based.
4. Databases on CD-ROM or other form of disc which can be searched by the library on its own microcomputer.

Besides this, there is an area of electronic networks which tie together the libraries and can be operated by individuals out of their homes or office.

TYPES OF REFERENCE SERVICE AVAILABLE ONLINE

Types of information services online varied greatly. Many types of searches are possible many times more than with manual methods. The following are some of the types of searches that can be done using online services:

1. Retrospective Search.

It is a common search which goes back to the earliest uates covered for one or more databases. A retrospective search may cover a specific topic, a certain author, a specific document type, a specific journal or some other particular area, but more often it is exhaustive.

2. Comprehensive Search

Comprehensive search is usually done on a specific topic. It typically covers all documents types, all author and all time periods covered by the appropriate databases. For examples a comprehensive search may pertain to patents, government activities, legislation etc. It also ensures exhaustivity.

3. Selective Search

By selective search means a bibliography of recent research about a specific author or ongoing research conducted by a specific organization. A list of newspaper articles on a recent event or on specific topic is another example. Online search is more amenable in such case than that of manual methods.

4. State-of-the Art Search

The state-of-the art search identifies the current status of an area of research in a particularly industry. It helps to discover what an organization or individual is doing presently.

5. SDI Search

Online SDI (Selective Dissemination of Information) search is considered ideal. A search profile can be stored indefinitely on an online retrieval system and search profile is updated automatically on many databases. The user simply enters the profile and citations are retrieved, then automatically mailed periodically to the user.

6. Ready-Reference Search

Many quick-reference questions can be answered by using online services. This is because online data-bases contain large amount of primary information in machine-readable form. Bibliographic data-bases may be used for citation verification for interlibrary loan purpose. Directory or numeric, textual type databases available online provide immediate answer.

7. Patent Search

Patent search is popular in business, commercial and industrial libraries. Manual patent search is highly time consuming and labour-intensive. Online patent search takes far less time and is less expensive. Patent issues and applications are both searchable.

Online reference services reviewed as above, are commonly met by the users in the libraries. There are many other types of searches that may be performed using online data-bases. Vendors like DIALOG, BRS, SDC and others can provide long list of online reference services available with them.

Advantages

Tedd discusses some of the advantages of this online approach for the librarians. They are briefly described as follow:

1. Immediate access to a wide range of information running into millions of records is possible.
2. The larger number of access points provide more effective and exhaustive search. It offers coordinate

terms, freetext searching and many other features which allow the searcher to go beyond the subject and/or another approach. Here Boolean logic operates.

3. Automatic printing of retrieved references (citations) and the ability to order a copy of the original document eliminates clerical hurdles.

4. Since online databases are readily updated than the printed version, currency automatically prevails.

5. Searching is much faster and response instantaneous.

6. Some databases are available online which have no equivalent printed product.

BIBLIOGRAPHIC SEARCH SERVICES

A number of notable online bibliographic search services are available. Some are discussed here briefly.

BLAISE

The British Library Automated Information Service (BLAISE) was introduced in 1977. It is a cataloguing service which includes both current and retrospective online access to UK and LC MARC records. Together the files contain over two million bibliographic records of books and serials. In addition to this, access to databases such as British Education Index and Eighteenth Century Short Title Catalogue is provided. This whole online search service is known as BLAISE - LINE and is used by libraries all over the world.

BRS

Bibliographic Retrieval Services (BRS) was introduced in 1976 in New York. The purpose was to provide innovative and cost-effective online search services. Its major service provides online access to bibliographic and full-text databases (mainly scientific and technical). Other services include facilities for the design, development and maintenance of private files and the design and implementation of specialist information retrieval software. BRS offers SDI service. It also makes available a cross data base for multifile searching, online accounting and an online catalogue service. It is owned by Information Handling Services.

ESA-IRS

The Information Retrieval Service (IRS) of the European Space Agency (ESA) at Frascati, Italy offers online search service in the early 1970s via a special telecommunications network-ESANET. Previously it used ESA/RECON, but the present software used is known as QUEST. The ESA-IRS database system provides access via online process to more than twenty databases mainly on nuclear and space sciences. In Britain, the Department of Industry has provided a dial-up technical information service known as DIAL TECH. ESA-IRS is one of the most used search services available on Euronet.

DIALOG

The DIALOG information retrieval service is run by Lockheed Information Services at Palo Alto in California. It is one of the first online search services which started operation in 1972. The search software was prepared from the RECON (Remote Console) developed by Lockheed for the National Aeronautics and Space Agency USA. The online services of DIALOG comprise 175 databases of which half can be categorised as scientific and technical. The other half includes subjects like, agriculture, humanities, social sciences, the arts, management, business, economics and information science etc. It has databases, both bibliographic and nonbibliographic, American and European. It charges access fee, telecommunication charges and prices for printouts of retrieved citations. Some of the databases are AGRICOLA, LISA SOCIAL SCISEARCH, COMPENDEX, ERIC etc. DIALOG has made tremendous contribution to online service in Europe. It contains over 16 million bibliographic citations available online and these are constantly reviewed and updated. It has online current awareness and SDI services.

SDC ORBIT

The System Development Corporation (SDC) started offering an online search service in 1972. Located at Sauta Monica, California, SDC and the Lockheed's Dialog are the largest online database organization in the world. Currently SDC has about eighty databases which cover a wide variety of subjects such as business and economics, chemistry, engineering, electronics, energy and environment, industrial science, petroleum and fossil fuels, US government reports and legislation, patents and social sciences. SDC prepared a software package for online search in 1968. It is known as ORBIT (Online Retrieval of Bibliographic Information Time-shared) some of the well known databases available through ORBIT are ACCOUNTANTS, AGRICOLA, BIOSIS, CHEMDEX, ENVIROLINE, ERIC, INSPEC, TITUS etc. Both DIALOG and ORBIT can be accessed via Telenet, Tymenet and other networks.

ORBIT also offers certain special services. These include SDI service and the facilities for users to establish and maintain their own private databases.

In addition to the few discussed above, several other online information systems in the United States have been developed. OCLC (Online Computer Library Centre) BALLOTS (Bibliographic Automation of Large Library Operations using a Time-sharing system) at Standford University, WLN (Washington Library Network at Olympia, RLIN (Research Libraries Information Network) are few examples. In Canada the largest online computerized library system is UTLAS (University of Toronto Library Automation). In Britain, the largest online system is BLAISE. It offers online services through a large number of databases under various names and styles, such as MEDLINE, SDI-LINE, TOXLINE, CHEMLINE, CANCERLINE. The second longest online system in the United Kingdom is called BLCMP (Birmingham Libraries Cooperative Mechanisation Project.) In Europe, online access is available to

ESA (European Space Agency) and DIMDI (Deutsches Institute for Medizinische Dokumentation and Information).

TYMNET AND TELENET

The member libraries to online search services as discussed above or any institution willing to pay the fees are using the online databases. No special telephone lines are required. The conventional telephone network provides access. But this dial-up method is recommended for those libraries which are located in the geographic vicinity of the given online database. For long distance communication, the use of online database by the libraries was expensive.

This obstacle was partially overcome during 1970s with introduction of publicly accessible packet-switching networks such as TYMNET and TELENET. Telenet and Tymnet are computer-controlled networks consisting of leased telephone lines which link geographically dispersed time-sharing computer services with access nodes in major and medium-sized cities. For example a library in New York wishing to access the DIALOG computer at Palo Alto in California, would dial a local Telenet or Tymnet telephone number and type a series of commands. This will cause the network's computers to route the call to the DIALOG computer. In most cases, Telenet and Tymnet charges are considerably lower than those incurred in conventional long-distance telephone communication. They have over 200 nodes in Europe and other parts of the world. Both provide access to almost all the major American online service. EURONET provides online service to EEC countries mainly but it is being extended to other countries also by interconnecting with the host computer systems of such countries.

Document Delivery Systems

By document delivery means the process in which libraries provide to the users the books articles, reports and other documents indexed in online databases, albeit in most of the cases it consists of citations and abstracts rather than the full text of the requested material. However to make the service complete the libraries have to evolve mechanism which enable them to deliver a document or a photo copy of the desired material into the users hand. The conventional interlibrary loan systems are highly time-consuming which offset the very purpose of online search. It is not unusual for U.S. Libraries to process backlogs of several days or even weeks and respond to those requests by means of efficient postal services. Thus in order to expedite the services it is thought necessary to investigate means of either supplying hard copy ordered during the search and retrieval process or supplying the full text as part of the retrieval process.

It is well realized that in the long run, the keys to more rapid document delivery will be the expansion of online databases to include full text of documents and the use of other technologies such as optical disc, either in conjunction with or apart from online delivery. The trend toward online full-text database is already evident.

As Reynolds has pointed out that online full-text databases are not now nor will they ever be an all-encompassing solution to the problem of document delivery in libraries. The current publications might be available online, there will still be large amount of retrospective materials published only in hard copy not converted to machine-readable form.

To address this problem consistent efforts have been made toward the development of alternative document delivery methodologies. For this purpose, several avenues have been attempted to facilitate library resources sharing activities. Efforts are also made to improve and speed up interlibrary loan processing through technological intervention. Also many libraries have sought solution in the use of COM to provide more convenient and speedy access to documents.

The present situation is that libraries are interested in more efficient and faster means of documents delivery at a time when full-text online databases and other advanced technologies are only beginning to address those needs. Libraries are using two methods to secure documents from remote locations. These are commercial document delivery service and digital telefacsimile technology. Many library consortia have established formal or informal courier services for document delivery. (Reynolds).

The need to send message speedily and accurately, telex systems are widely used which are invariably known as electronic mail, electronic messaging or teletex. Teletex is an enhanced telex system. A teletex terminal is a device similar to a word processor with a keyboard, screen, printer and internal storage. Some word processors, such as IBM's Display writer, are capable of receiving and transmitting teletex data. Project Hermes established in 1984 is a teletex-based document-delivery service which incorporates: document ordering, automatic document delivery, regular delivery of pre-specified documents, electronic mail, transfer of documents between participants.

Another technique which is used for document delivery is telefacsimile which is also known as facsimile or fax. There are both analog and digital facsimile machines and facsimile can be sent via cable, telephone lines, microwave and other means. Usually they are sent over telephone lines because that is more economical.

Another latest device is known as LDX (Long Distance Xerox). It is a telefacsimile system which provides 135 lines per inch and electrostatic printing on paper. Only single pages (not directly from books) can be transmitted. It is costly but is speedy one.

From an operator's point of view, the procedure for transmitting copies on a digital machine is similar to that required for the analog modules. A page of a document is placed on a surface similar in appearance to the surface of a photocopying machine. After a telephone connection has been established with the receiving site, the sending machine scans a page and converts the image into electronic signals, which are transmitted over the telephone line to the machine at the receiving site. A facsimile of the original is produced in hard-copy form based on the pattern of signals received. Digital telefacsimile machine can transmit an image of a page in less than 60 seconds. Although not widely used in libraries, it is being experimented as a means of document delivery in US and Europe.

There are several other electronic document delivery systems being planned. A consortium of five major publishers comprising Elsevior, Pergaman, Wiley, Academic, Springer and Black-Wells Scientific planned to implement a system under the name of ADONIS (Article Delivery Over Network Information Systems). Started in 1981 it aimed to supply facsimile images of pages from Video disc. It uses a combination of láser scanning and printing, and digital optical storage of the complete page of scientific, technical and medical journal articles. Requests for copies are sent to Adonis from the BLLD (British Library Lending Division).

The future of telefacsimile in the libraries is not bright since it is too expensive and the quality of reproduction is still not good nor is there a real need to provide document so rapidly. Above all, in the light of recent trend toward online full-text database, telefacsimile is considered an outdated technology.

Select Bibliography

Bourne, C.P. "On-Line Systems: History, Technology, Economics". *Journal of the American Society for Information Science* 31: 155-60 (May, 1980).

Collinge, B. "Blaise - The British Library Automated Information Service". *ASLIB Proceedings*. 30: 394-402 (Nov. 1978).

Cooper, M. D. "Charging Users for Library Services". *Information Processing and Management* 10: 304-19 (Spring, 1977).

Hawkins, D. T. Online Information Retrieval Systems. In Annual Review of Information Science and Technology, edited by M.E. Williams. White Plains, N.Y: Knowledge Industries Publications, 1981.

Houghton, B. & Convey, J. Online Information Retrieval System. 2nd ed. London: Clive Bingley, 1984.

Katz, William A. Introduction to Reference Works, 5th ed. New York: McGraw Hill, 1987.

Kent, A., and Galvin, T. J. The On-Line Revolution in Libraries. New York: Marcel Dekker, 1978.

Pollitt, A. S. Information Storage and Retrieval System: Origin, Development and Applications. Chichester: Ellis Horwood, 1989.

Reynold Dennis. Library Automation: Issues and Applications. New York: R. R. Bowker, 1985.

Rowley, Jennifer E. Computers for Libraries. New York: C. Bingley, 1980.

Salton, Gerard & McGill, Nichael J. Introduction to Modern Information Retrieval. New York: McGraw-Hill, 1983.

Tedd, L. "Computer based information retrieval services". Handbook of Special Librarianship and Information Work. London, Aslib, 1982.

Tedd, Lucy A. An Introduction to Computer-based Library Systems. 2nd ed. new York: John Wiley, 1984.

CHAPTER 9

Automated Acquisitions

The term acquisition commonly denotes procurement of library materials which are published on nonrecurring basis including books, technical reports, government publications, and audiovisual materials. The acquisition of journals, magazines and other periodicals literature is considered a facet of serials control. A separate chapter is therefore devoted to study automated serials control.

Libraries in the United States had introduced automated acquisitions as early as 1959 using for book ordering systems like keypunch equipment, card sorters, and tabulating machine. In the early 1960s, batch-processing, computer-based acquisitions systems were developed by a number of academic libraries. In the late 1960s and early 1970s, several academic libraries in U.S. implemented online acquisitions systems-the most widely known being the Book Order and Selection System (BOSS). Despite these promising initiatives automated acquisitions systems failed to attract the widespread library and vendor interest. However interest in automated acquisition increased steadily since the late 1970s. In the 1980s, there are in U.S. a variety of organizations such as cooperative systems, booksellers, as well as integrated software packages and turnkey system which are used to assist acquisition work.

Automated acquisition is immensely significant for the libraries. It provides a base to computerize other library activities without much labour. It contributes to the development of integrated libraries systems in which a single bibliographic data base serves the various information-processing requirements of technical services, references and administrative applications. Bibliographic data held in machine-readable form can later be increased or modified to support circulation, cataloguing or other library activities eliminating duplication of work routines.

Functions Of Acquisition Section

A good ordering and acquisition system may comprise the following activities:

1. Receiving records of items for acquisitions.
2. Ascertaining whether those items are already in the library or in the order procedure. If items are in the library, how many additional copies are to be ordered. If previous editions are there, what are the identities of new editions recommended for the order.
3. Making input of the order in the specified format.
4. Checking whether orders are overdue and, if so, chasing the supplier and sending reminders.
5. Checking of invoices or bills, if supplied.
6. Accounting under fund heads and sending bills for payment.
7. Maintaining record files for items on order.
8. Accessioning of items received.
9. Maintaining the accounts.
10. Keeping statistics.
11. Updating the whole record to ensure the latest position from time to time.
12. Maintaining the master file of orders and acquisitions. (Mahapatra)

BOOK ORDER FORMAT IN AUTOMATED SYSTEM

A format of the book order comprising basic information is given below:

Order number and date

ISBN
Author
Title and edition
Publisher and date of publication
Price
Fund head
Number of copies
Bookseller or vendor
Stipulated date within which supply should be made.

The data field of the International Standard Book Number (ISBN) is a fixed one. Data fields of other information may vary in length from item to item. Therefore, the record structure for the order system must be specific and this can be determined by the strings of bits.

The accuracy of bibliographical details is most essential in an automated acquisition system. ISBN can help in this respect. While the items have been received and acquisition made, a batch of printouts may be used for various record purposes, such as cataloguing records, book cards for the circulation section etc.

Books are also received through gift or exchange. In these cases, certain computer operations are not required. The ordering function, the chasing function, the accounts and billing functions are eliminated. But these items have to be recorded on receipt and accessioned accordingly. Statistics should be kept as these are vital part of the library holdings.

INPUT

Whether selection of material and verification of bibliographic data, etc., is carried out manually or by automated methods, it is essential that ordering and related bibliographic information is converted to machine-readable form for entry into a computer-maintained master acquisition file. The following data is generally input to the computer to perform the above mentioned functions in local library setup.

1. Data regarding new orders. (Bibliographic detail)
2. Revisions or amendments to orders placed.
3. Position, whether received or not.
4. Whether reminders have been sent, if not received?
5. Records of received books.
6. Records of acquisitions.
7. Records of accounts.

OUTPUT

The output data of the computer for ordering and acquisition functions include the following:

1. Printouts of the items ordered, to be sent to the booksellers directly.
2. Printouts of items ordered, but not received.
3. Printed reminders to booksellers.
4. Accession records.
5. Book cards for the circulation section.
6. Bibliographic records used for catalogue records.
7. Processing slips.
8. Accounts under fund heads for budget control as well as current state of different budget heads.
9. Statistics of various natures.
10. Printout lists of recently acquired items.
11. Processed data of any kind relating to ordering, acquisitions and the analysis of data for decision-making.
12. Any data required for the integrated computer system. (Mahapatra)

FINANCIAL CONTROL FUNCTIONS

The library manager and the accounts section greatly benefit from the improved accounting control over library activities through computer. By maintaining fund file the benefits accrued are as follow.

1. The computer automatically conveys information to accounts department about payments made or to be made.

2. The computer prints an exception message if placing a particular order exceeds the appropriation or budget for an account or project.

3. The computer system keeps up-to-date records of budget allocations . by department, branch library, section, project, type of material or any other accounting breakdowns.

4. The computer keeps accurate and current accounting records including amounts spent by divisions or departments of the budget, dates spent, balance available, and totals as needed.

5. The computer keeps accurate and current records of the balance of deposits where advance payments have been made.

In most libraries, the format of the accounting data files are governed by the requirements of the accounting department or section. It is the duty of the systems analyst to design library information system in line with the requirements of the accounting department. Generally, at the time of order, the computer should transfer to the accounting department the amount of money to be paid on prepaid orders and to be paid after delivery. This enables accounting department to keep up-to-date records of uncommitted budget.

OTHER AUTOMATED FUNCTIONS

1. The computer can be used to identify and print follow-up reminders for incomplete processes, unpaid invoices, overdue orders, violations of processing rule and other control checks.

2. Computer can monitor processing work. It can record items that have been received but not catalogued. If the

computer prints out listings of such items at frequent intervals, they can serve multipurpose for the staff and the users of the collection.

3. The computer may be used to keep accurate records of the number of orders and receipts processed, by whom, to what vendors, etc. These records provide library management with complete information on the acquisitions department workload. On the basis of this, reports can be prepared weekly, monthly, or as needed to count and summarize the types and number of documents, transactions, etc., processed.
4. If desired, computer can prepare lists of all orders placed each day and register all items received each day. It can be an essential tool in maintaining control of the acquisitions process.
5. As previously indicated most automated acquisition systems have the ability to print claiming and cancellation notices to vendors at predetermined intervals and also arrival notices to the requesters when items are received in the library.

RELATIONSHIP TO CATALOGUING ACTIVITIES

After the acquisition function has been automated, much of the data needed for cataloguing the item, is available to the computer in machine-readable form. Title, author, publisher, date of publication, corporate authors, technical report numbers, etc. have all been Keyed in either at the point of ordering or at the point of receipt. The computer can prepare a cataloguing worksheet for the professional cataloguer containing all the information entered up to the point of cataloguing. In order to complete cataloguing process, the professional librarian provides subject headings, assigns a call number, and reviews the work done by acquisition section. The cataloguer may also modify or correct any item of information from cataloguing viewpoint. A well-designed computer system should have the ordering/receiving data feed automatically into the cataloguing subsystem, thereby relieving the cataloguer from labour duplication.

DATA FILES

A computer based acquisition system warrants at least three different files as detailed below:

1. **Main Order File.** It is usually arranged by the order number. Here the order number is the key for access to any record kept in the computer. This file should be kept updated with the changes either in the bibliographical record, or in the price record, or in the actual cost record, or in any other respect immediately.

2. **Vendor File.** This file contains the name and addresses of the vendors (booksellers) used by the library. The purpose is to save labour. Vendor code can be used on the order record. The vendor file with the assigned codes generally contains the following data elements:

    1. Vendor code number.
    2. Vendor's name and address.
    3. Telephone number.
    4. Telex number.
    5. Cable/Gram.
    6. Currency accepted.

3. **Requester File.** This file is essential because, the requester number is to be recorded in the order file. Whenever the document is received in the library, intimation is sent to the requester. The requester file generally consists of the following data elements:

    1. Requester Number
    2. User's Name
    3. User's address
    4. Telephone number, etc.

Outstanding purchase orders file is also maintained by certain libraries. It contains all items ordered but not yet received.

Whenever books are received, the computer held order record is amended immediately. The receipt of books is recorded in the acquisition part and the order records for such books is closed. The reported delay in supply of books may be added to the record in the coded form indicating that the order remains outstanding for certain reasons.

It is better to make additions, deletion, amendments or corrections to the order file in batch-processing and to monitor progress of work done and financial situation at intervals of short duration. Obviously, the whole work design and operations depend on the capability of the computer, computer hardware and software.

COMPUTER - BASED ACQUISITION ALTERNATIVES.

Apart from using local automated acquisition systems and transfer of software from one library to another, there are four principal sources of acquisitions systems on the market of U.S. and other technologically advanced countries today.

These four different alternatives are: (1) Customed-developed (inhouse self-made) acquisition software package; (2) Library can purchase turnkey system or prewritten commercially available acquisitions specific software package; (3) acquisition application module within a multifunction integrated library system; (4) Online, service offered by a bibliographic utility or a book jobbers to be accessed by the subscribers on time-sharing basis.

Custom-developed System

The custom-developed acquisitions systems may be executed on a computer owned and operated by the library itself.

These may be centralized computers operated by a university, parent body or other organization with which the library is affiliated. This has one important advantage: hardware components can be selected & programs written to the library's own specifications. But this is a highly time-consuming and expensive activity that can result in delays. As a result this system is usually viewed as an implementation alternative as last resort.

Prewritten Or Turnkey Systems

The purchase of turnkey systems or prewritten acquisitions software can minimize the worst effects of customized system. Prewritten programs are invariably designed for use on a particular hardware (computer) equipped with specific systems software. Libraries are therefore bound to obtain prewritten acquisition software compatible with their existing computer installation. But they are available with commercial vendors.

A prewritten acquisitions program may be purchased as a stand-alone product or as one component in a more comprehensive, multifunctional library automation software package. As an example, the ACQ 350 Acquisitions System from OCLC operates on the OCLC M300 workstation and other IBM-compatible microcomputer systems. (Saffady).

Acquisition-specific turnkey products consist of preconfigured combination of hardware and prewritten software sold as a single system. But recently, the most sophisticated, multipurpose turnkey systems have been developed. In addition to their use for acquisition purpose, they have some other capabilities. They can store MARC record; interface with most bibliographic utilities. They are fit for circulation control, online catalogue access systems; can print a wide variety of reports including lists of titles under review for ordering and orders requested by specific persons; and transmits orders electronically to various booksellers.

Multifunction Integrated System

An integrated system is one in which several functions share a common database and all functions can be accessed using a common sign-on and related commands.

As another alternative, a number of multifunctional library automation software packages and turnkey integrated systems are available. In this group, the integration of acquisitions with cataloguing and circulation in a single system offers several advantages. But these systems do not provide direct access to large generalized bibliographic databases as do the utilities or book jobbers. Examples include, Geac library automation systems; the NOTIS software package; the DOBIS/LIBIS software package from IBM.

All of these approaches require a substantial capital investment which can be minimized if automated acquisitions capabilities are obtained on a time-sharing basis through a bibliographic utility or book jobber. It is sometime advised to the libraries in United States either to adopt the integrated system offered by the Utility or have "interface" arrangement with book jobbers.

BIBLIOGRAPHIC UTILITY SYSTEMS

All the four of the major North American Utilities such as OCLC, RLIN, WLN, and UTLAS, offer online acquisition systems to member libraries. They have the large databases of bibliographic record on which a library can draw upon. They offer acquisitions components that are tied in with their bibliographic databases, allowing for the transfer of certain types of information from existing bibliographic records directly onto the order records being created by individual libraries. All the four online acquisition systems are discussed here briefly.

OCLC (Online Computer Library Centre)

OCLC "Acquisition Subsystem" provides access to the Online Union Catalog from which orders may be generated. There is an online in-process file, automatic transfer of constant data (i.e. bibliographic information) to other online files, fund accounting and report generation, as well as receipt and claiming. As of 1984, orders were mailed to the vendor since no direct transmission of orders to vendor was available. But now the ACQ 350 Acquisitions System of OCLC can communicate with the OCLC online union catalog for the bibliographic verification and electronic order transmission (Saffady).

RLIN (Research Libraries Information Network)

RLIN II (the acquisition module) is available to libraries through California Library Authority for Systems and Services (CLASS). It is a comprehensive system from verification to receipt of item and direct accessions etc. Fiscal aspect is not covered. Verification is done online. It allows access to member library not only to its own holding records but also the holdings of the Library of Congress and the 200 member libraries. Through RLIN's system, a member library can maintain, in the acquisition system, not only a record of titles ordered, but also titles considered and rejected. Orders are still mailed to the appropriate vendor/jobber by the library. Direct electronic order placement with a vendor is not possible at this time.

WLN (Washington Library Networks)

"Acquisition Subsystem" consists of four files in-process, standing orders, name and address, and account status. These files, combined with cataloguing files, allow the library to operate and maintain acquisitions records for an item from selection to "on the shelf status". It handles both individual and standing order transactions. An order is created by entering the order command and a purchase order number, after finding the appropriate bibliographic record in the data base. This automatically links the orders to the "Bibliographic File" and causes a formatted order screen to be displayed. It is also possible to create an order record which is not linked to the Bibliographic File. Once the necessary order information has been added to the "In-process File" record, a purchase order can be printed, or the order can be routed directly to any vendor using the WLN On-line Transmission of Orders facility. Purchase orders, are printed or routed automatically to vendors three times a week. But Saffady reports that, at present, the system provides overnight electronic transmission to several dozen booksellers. The record can be updated online using individual commands and formatted screens. Bibliographic information can be added, deleted, or altered in "In-process File" records without affecting the "Bibliographic File."

UTLAS (The University of Toronto Library Automation System)

In Canada this is a regional library network. The UTLAS system (Online Acquisitions control System) is similar to the other bibliographic utilities in that the basic functions are covered-verification to payment. What is special about this system and WLN is that, unlike RLIN, it is possible to place many orders electronically: "speedier service through electronic communication with vendors holding UTLAS vendor accounts." Another unique feature of UTLAS is its international scope; the bibliographic data base for verification covers much more than American publishers' output and publication in the English language.

BOOK JOBBER SERVICES

A large number of booksellers and library suppliers are now offering online access to their databases. These organizations typically started to use computer systems to run their own ordering and supplying processes during the 1970s, usually beginning with a file of stock titles only but now have built large MARC-based bibliographic records. Most of these services are accessible using teletype-compatible terminals which might also be used for carrying out online searches on DIALOG etc.

Baker & Taylor and Brodart in United States are the largest book jobbers-which maintain a large bibliographic database, although not as large as do the Utilities. They have several automated acquisition systems available: LIBRIS II is a system tied into the Baker & Taylor mainframe computer system and several variations under Bata SYSTEMS are designed to allow libraries to use their own computer systems. LIBRIS II allows searching a data base of 350,000 titles created by Baker & Taylor. The database is updated weekly. Orders can be generated online and electronic order placement to Baker & Taylor is possible. The system allows for fund accounting and is capable of retaining both the current and previous years' budgets for reconciliation purposes. A warning system is incorporated to protect overspending. The system can be used to print orders for other vendors.

Brodart's OLAS system is accessed on a time-sharing basis through terminals located in subscribing libraries. It requires minimal capital investment in equipment. OLAS users may pay a monthly or annual subscription fee for unlimited connect time or incur connect time charges based on actual usage. Brodart maintains a substantial database which can be searched online for bibliographic verification. The user has the ability to transmit orders electronically to vendor.

TELEORDERING

Tedd records another development seen in UK which links the publishing and bookselling trades in Teleordering. Intelligent terminals in bookshops are used to record details of orders, using their ISBNs. This information is sent via the telephone to the Teleordering computer system where the ISBNs are checked against Whitaker's British Books in Print database and the full author/title details are retrieved and order to the publishers are despatched. The advantages include cost savings, less errors, improved reporting and speedier distribution, all of which affect the acquisitions system in a library.

BIBLIOGRAPHIC DATABASES

Quite a number of machine-readable databases are found in the market. Books in Print database is available through several online search services. It is a machine-readable counterpart of several printed trade bibliographics. Bowker has introduced a CD-ROM implementation of BOOKS IN PRINT PLUS and BOOK REVIEWS PLUS.

In U.S. the Library Corporation has introduced the Book Indentification and Ordering System which is a microcomputer-based CD-ROM system designed for bibliographic verification and book ordering. It features the ANY-BOOK data base of English-Language titles available from over 22000 publishers. Menu-driven software permits searches by author, title, ISBN, or LC card number. Retrieved records are displayed as order-form images containing bibliographic and ordering information. When the operator enters additional ordering information, the system automatically calculates prices, checks for items already on order, and prints order forms. It can also transmit orders electronically to designated publishers or jobbers. (Saffady).

Select Bibliography

Boss, Richard. Automating Library Acquisitions: Issues and Outlook. New York: Knowledge Industry Pub. 1982.

Lovecy, Ian. Automating Library Procedures: a Survior's Handbook. London: The Library Association 1984.

Mahapatra Piyushkanti, Dr. The Computer in Library Service. Calcutta: The World Press, 1985.

Reynolds Dennis. Library Automation: Issues and Applications. New York: R. R. Bowker, 1985.

Rice James. Introduction to Library Automation. Littleton: Libraries Unlimited, 1984.

Saffady, William, "Library Automation: an Overview," *Library Trends* 37: 269-81 (Winter 1989).

Swihart, S. J. and Hefley, B. F. Computer Systems in the Library. Los Angeles: Melville Pub. 1973.

Tedd, Lucy A. An Introduction to Computer-based Library Systems. 2nd ed. New York: John Wiley, 1984.

CHAPTER *10*

Automated Serials Control

The problem of controlling serials by computer remained a challenge for a long time. Some believed that it was one of the most difficult housekeeping operations to be automated mainly due to the unpredictable nature of serial publications. Serials control systems are indeed distinct from monograph systems in a number of ways. A monograph is a single entity at hand whereas serials are published at regular or irregular intervals; their contents usually vary from issue to issue. An article as a single bibliographic unit may be published in more than one issue and even in more than one volume. Secondly an issue of a serial may not be a bibliographic unit in itself but a bibliographic unit embodied in a particular article comprising more than one issue or volume. Obviously, users may be interested in an issue of a serial as a bibliographic unit or an article spread over a number of issues as a bibliographic unit. This conflict between the physical unit and the bibliographic unit and their management problem make serials control a complex task. Thus this very complexity kept computerized serials-control lagged behind from that of monographs.

Computers were first used to assist in the control of serials in the 1960s. The systems depended on punched cards and batch processed. Even today the majority of the automated serials control are batch processed run on a mainframe computer. In 1970s a number of libraries in the U.S. attempted online real-time integrated serials control systems. Many developments are now seen in this area. The serial services are being offered by library cooperatives, and special serial subscription agencies. More software for serial control are being developed.

AUTOMATED SERIAL CONTROL SYSTEM

Computerised serials control system comprises several subsystems. They are:

1. INVENTORY - Preparation of lists of serials in cards and to make input to the computer, designing and implementation of data files.
2. ORDERING AND ACQUISITION - Selection, ordering and acquisition of serials newly subscribed.
3. ACCESSIONS - Receiving of serials, checking-in, placing claims if not received, renewal of subscription, checking gaps, if any, updating of holding records, placing orders for back volumes, preparation of data files, record maintenance, etc.
4. CATALOGUING - Preparation of catalogues of serials and other records designed to meet the needs of users.
5. CIRCULATION - Making available serials issues in separate volumes in the bound form, keeping records of circulation, checking and making arrangements for binding, preparation of lists of titles or lists of articles, etc. (Mahapatra)

Inventory

Inventories of serials may be prepared primarily in the card form under the title and the subject with cross references from previous files, if any. Each title is recorded by the date of the first volume and subsequent volumes indicating any missing issues. Location is indicated by the call number given to periodical title or the shelf mark. While inventories are prepared in any form as required in the individual library, these may be edited and recorded in the required format. The records then may be kept in the computer in punched cards, or magnetic tape or disk. The magnetic tape file may be sorted for preparing various kins of inventories and printout obtained from the computer.

Once main files or database files are input to the computer, updating with keypunching will be simpler and easier. The updating of input data may be of three kinds- additions, deletions, and changes. Higher degree of accuracy is achieved by the computer.

Ordering And Acquisition

The initial ordering of a serial is akin to ordering a monograph. Ordering entails processes like requesting, approving, checking, ordering and accounting in respect of each new serial title.

In the accounting system, the total amount of money to be spent on serial is usually called the serials fund which is divided among subjects or departments. The serials fund is further sub-divided under a number of heads, such as back-sets and duplicate volumes purchases, and binding etc. Financial data file is maintained which shows in general two kinds of transactions- (1) those made under each head and (2) those made with each of the suppliers and/or the parties with whom any transaction is made. New orders are input to computer with all details of price, cost invoice, amount paid or ready for payment.

The acquisitions function may be divided into two parts i.e. receiving and claiming. When an issue is received, it must be checked to ensure that this is the correct or latest item received and then the main data file must be amended to show new receipts. Typically a file of punched cards should be created for all the serials to be received. When the issue arrives the card file is searched and extracted and a new card prepared if no appropriate card is present in the file. All cards relevant to the issues received are eventually processed in a batch and the computer-held main data file is updated. The remaining cards, if any, serve to alert the librarian to the non-receipt of certain issues. (J.E. Rowley).

The claiming function is a smaller but a complex job. The point at which the claiming procedures should start, mainly depends upon the professional judgment of the librarian. The computer easily provides list of outstanding issues that the librarian needs in order to send claims.

Preparing record for renewal of subscription is a routine job. The data file for acquisitions may include the details of the dates when subscriptions fall due to be renewed and the amounts to be paid. The printouts of such records may be produced at regular intervals for perusal and action. Renewal notices may be printed by the computer. After making payment in each case of renewal, the account to show balance should be updated. Computer can provide printed lists of the financial situation which are a useful management tool.

Accessions

Each new issue of the serial is recorded in the library. If it is a new serial, it should be input to the data file with bibliographic detail. When all the records are input and the files are updated, the issue may be sent to the reading room or the place where to send. The next useful job which is performed by the computerised accessioning subsystem is the production of a current list of recent arrivals of journals. It may be used as a part of current awareness service.

Integrated System

It may be mentioned that in computer- based networks (e.g. OCLC, WLN or RLIN) ordering, acquisition or check-in system depends upon centrally located full bibliographic data base. The member libraries use this facility only through their nodes. They are directed to adhere strictly to the practice/standard approved by the system and create files accordingly at their respective centres.

Cataloguing

In an automated serials Cataloguing Work, the bibliographic data is recorded in machine-readable form. As stated earlier computer-based serials system generates, from the master file, lists in several orders, e.g. title, subject, location, supplier, etc. Here, there is no difference between a monograph and serial automated work. Then the serials catalogues may be printed in book-form or COM. The frequency of updating the lists varies but usually lies between the limits defied by monthly and annually. (J.E. Rowley).

Circulation And Binding

Circulation of serials is practised on limited scale. For an ordinary loan circulation-control system for monograph can suffice for serials. However routing of serials is important in special library and must be computerized. To operate such a system a list of users, their location, department and details of the serials they would like to see are input and lists of readers for each issue of a serial are produced. Ideally the list should be produced in an order which minimizes the movement of an issue between different departments and locations and also reflects the priorities. The bound issues or back-sets of a serial may be loaned to readers in some libraries. The technique for circulation is usually the same as for lending books.

Binding

The primary objectives of automated bindery control include:

1. Production of binding slip.
2. Identification of volumes ready to bind.
3. A record of volumes at the bindery from which the volumes not returned on schedule may be identified.

The computer-based bindery control modules are either part of an automated check-in system or are a standalone (local) bindery control system. Each bindery system works slightly different. In all cases, however, binding slips or lists are produced to accompany the volumes sent to the bindery. These binding slips and/or lists are created from records which generally contain the following data: title (or author and title), binding colour, class of binding, colour of lettering and its style, size and location (for title, volume, and call number), instructions for handling advertisements, indexes, and title page. Most of the systems have the binding data coded in fixed length fields. Some bindery records also contain issue, frequency, number of issues bound together, and binding frequency.

The identification of the volumes to be bound can be accomplished automatically using the issue frequency and the number of issues bound together or using the frequency of binding. Several bindery control systems allow the production of binding slips (lists) on request. These systems allow the request as part of the serial check-in system.

The third function of a bindery control system is to provide a record of volumes at the bindery. This record is made accessible by call number and title as well as the bindery shipment. Online circulation systems can be used to charge volumes to the bindery and to provide overdue notices when volumes at the bindery are not returned on schedule.

The Control System

All these subsystems must be integrated in one serials control system. Each of the subsystems must have a main file or master file and other working files. All these files must be integrated in one file in the serials control system which constitutes the core file. The core file is the master file of the system and all other files and records are subordinate to this core file. The central control, data record, decision making, management production of printouts in desired sequences, accounts, statistics and every routine and management job will be controlled by this system with the core file. It may be designated Master Serial Control File. It will hold all the records centrally with connections to the following data files - selection data, ordering data, acquisition data, accessioning data, cataloguing data, description data, circulation data, users data, binding data, binders data, suppliers data, holding data, statistical data, non-receiving data, accounting data, financial data, claims data, renewal data, cancellation data, etc. These data can produce printout lists for various purposes. (Mahapatra)

The core file should include the following information:

Identification number
International Standard Serial Number (ISSN)
Title and abbreviated title
Call number or shelf number
Frequency
Expected dates of receiving issues
Library holdings and wants
Volumes bound and unbound
Supplier
Subscription rate in rupees and foreign currency, if any
Subject (may be coded)
Language (may be coded)
Nature of the serial (whether abstracting or indexing journal or having other special feature). (Mahapatra).

For the serials control system, it is better to start with key punching and unit card methods. The punched cards in file or deck can be used. If possible, the paper tape and magnetic media can be used as with handling books etc. In serials control department batch-processing is the most convenient method for record and operation. But an online integrated system is highly desirable for all sorts of quick references.

INTERNATIONAL SERIALS CONTROL SYSTEMS

Computerisation in libraries has created immense potentialities in standardisation of data at the international level and opened up a new vista for transfer of and access to information and documents. The capabilities of the computer have been increased enormously. All these situations have contributed to making transfer of software packages across geographical barriers and national boundaries. Attempts have been being made for controlling data at the international level by the machine-readable form.

ISBD(s)

To create and maintain international standards in bibliographic descriptions for easy flow of information, IFLA started the programme of the International Standard Biblicgraphic Description (ISBD) to be applied to national bibliographies, library catalogues and other information sources. The aim of ISBD is to provide standard descriptions for library materials of different kinds, and to ensure international propagation of bibliographic information. The functions of ISBD's are to make records from different sources interchangeable, so that, records produced in one country can be easily accepted in library catalogues and/or other bibliographic lists in any other country and to assist in the interpretation of records transcending language barriers, so that records produced for users of one language can be interpreted by users of other languages. By the application of the International Standard Bibliographic Description, the bibliographic records can be converted to the machine-readable form. The bibliographic descriptions of serials are made by the International Standard Bibliographic Description (Serials), ISBD(S), which can be used in the machine-readable format.

ISSN

The use of International Standard Book Number (ISBN) in publications makes it possible to identify them. In countries where ISBN has been accepted, all the recent publications are marked with the International Standard Book Numbers. For identification, ordering and processing of serial publications, the International Standard Serial Number (ISSN) is being used.

There are many national centres established in different countries, and they register and allocate the International Standard Serial Numbers. These unique International Standard Serial Numbers (ISSN's) facilitate computerisation of serials catalogue records by providing machine-readable serials records. These ISSN's act as access points to the international network of serials publications. They also promote computer-based information service on the strength of holdings of serials in various libraries at the international level. (Mahapatra)

CODEN

ISSN is not the only serial numbering system. Twenty year older is CODEN system developed by the American Society for Testing and Materials, fully titled CODEN FOR PERIODICAL TITLES. It is controlled by the Chemical Abstracts Service and covers mainly scientific and technical literature. Details of titles covered are given in the INTERNATIONAL CODEN DIRECTORY. In a sense, of course, ISSN and CODEN are rivals; in practice, both are frequently cited on the same publication.

ISDS

The International Serial Data System (ISDS) was set up in 1971 under the world science information programme. UNISIST, recognising the fact that an internationally accepted coding system for serial was essential for machine-readable records. It was also felt that an effective system for compilation and dissemination of information on serials was essential. For these reasons an international centre, ISDS, was established in Paris. (Mahapatra)

THE INTERNATIONAL SERIAL DATA SYSTEM acts as a central node in an international network of national centres with the aim at meeting the need for an internationally accepted coding system for periodical titles for collecting, recording and disseminating accurate information on the periodical literature. The general aims of the ISDS are to:

1. Develop and maintain an international register of serial publications.
2. Define and promote the use of international standard serial numbers.
3. Facilitate the retrieval of scientific and technical information in serials.
4. Make this information currently available to all countries, organizations or individual users.
5. Establish a communications network between libraries, secondary information services, publishers of serial literature and international organizations.
6. Promote international standards for bibliographic descriptions, communication formats, and information exchange in the area of serials publications. (Tedd).

The International Serial Data System records conform to the MARC standards. It uniquely identifies the serial title whether the International Standard Serial Number has been used or not. The components of the ISDS are:

ISSN
Key title
Variant Title, if any
Abbreviated title
Imprint
Frequency
Country of origin
Former and later title, if any
Language edition, if any
Related title, if any

The ISDS records may be used in computer-based libraries. They are available in the MARC exchange format. The ISDS, ISBD(s) and ISSN have made serials control most effective and efficient both at the national and international levels. They too have promoted international exchange of information and software package transfer in the machine-readable form.

CONSER

Conversion of Serials Records project (CONSER) was initiated by the United States in 1974. Now it is a cooperative project undertaken by the Library of Congress, the National Library of Canada, the National Library of Medicine and the National Agricultural Library and other participating libraries. The retrospective and current serials records are being converted to the machine-readable form. The National Serial Database has been established in the Library of Congress, under the National Serial Data Programme (NSDP) as a part of CONSER. The serial database is accessible via the Online Computerised Library Centre (OCLC, formerly Ohio College Library Centre) network. CONSER records may be used in union lists, bibliographies, information retrieval and as a basis for selection and acquisition. Products available from CONSER includes: (a) weekly tapes of serials records; (b) a keyword-out of context index of serials titles; and (c) a microfiche of authenticated records. (Rowley)

SUBSCRIPTION AGENCY SERVICES

Many of the serials subscription agencies have started offering services to libraries to assist serials control. This is quite similar to the services being provided to assist libraries in the fields of ordering and acquisition of monographs. In Europe and U.S. many such agencies have developed inhouse computer-based systems for ordering, claiming and supplying their customer libraries with serials. Humphreys in Potter and Sirkin work "*Serials Automation in the U.S.*", categorizes the services offered by the subscription agencies in the following way:

1. Subscription handling. This is the primary service offered by the agencies. A basic subscription handling service includes contacting the publishers to determine

rates, ordering, preparing invoices and dealing with renewals.

2. Bibliographic information related to serials. This service is really a by-product of the subscription handling service. The quality of bibliographic data provided varies, and some agencies are considering acquiring the CONSER database. Some agencies provide the bibliographic data in a variety of physical forms and some provide online access.
3. Budgetary details. This includes providing libraries with details of expenditure on serials by fund account, budget code, subject parameters and so on.
4. Issue handling and check-in. This can either be carried out directly by the agency or software for this purpose may be developed by the agency for use on a library's inhouse computer system.
5. Production of union list. (Tedd).

The following four agencies are extensively providing subscription services to libraries in U.S., U.K. and elsewhere:

i. Ebsco, Birmingham, Alabama, U.S.
ii. Faxon, Massachusetts, U.S.
iii. Swets and Zeittinger, Lisse, Netherlands.
iv. Blackwell's Oxford, U.K.

COMPUTER CATALOGUING FOR SERIALS

Automation is doing a good deal with serials cataloguing data which facilities search and retrieval. There is complete access to everything in the record from all possible angles. This increase in access points per bibliographic item is a great achievement of computer in cataloguing work.

Cataloguing serials is now easier than ever before. It has solved many problems of automated serials cataloguing. A few relatively minor differences exist for descriptive cataloguing of monographs and serials. ISBD provides a framework for describing any type of material libraries collect. and that framework is the basis for Part 1 of AACR2. The rules laid down make cataloguing aspect of serial consistent with the description of other materials. The other part of descriptive cataloguing is the application of Part II of AACR2. These rules apply equally to any materials; seriality is no longer a factors. Moreover the use of computer has relegated the concept of main entry to background. It does not depend upon a particular entry point. A good consolation for serials cataloguers.

The bibliographic elements suggested in AACR2 as appropriate to serial cataloguing are confined to eight areas. The cataloguer does not face any problem in doing manual or automated serial cataloguing. The trouble arises with blending these entries in a computer system. The "entry" in a computer system may drive from a MARC record or from a CONSER (Conversion of Serials). Individual serials cataloguers may disagree on statements of responsibility, series formation, title proper, or other information in the area of description. Another point of interest is that if a serial is entered on MARC/CONSER record in a way which differs from local practice it is a must for local library using a system, to change the entry and adhere to the practice displayed in the data base being used, may it be CONSER or WLN or any other.

Osborn gives the following instructions to serials cataloguers.

1. Since AACR2 calls for inclusion of the ISSN and key title in the catalogue entry for serials, these should be followed.
2. Should CODEN or another symbol be employed, the other coding should be substituted for ISSN in the catalogue entry.
3. Key titles be recorded in abbreviated form. The standards employed in abstracting and indexing services can be adopted, otherwise recourse should be had to two

publications of the International Organization for Standardization: International Code for the Abbreviation of Title of Periodicals (Geneva 1972) and International List of Periodical Titles Word Abbreviations (Geneva 1973).

4. Abbreviated key titles should be followed for headings on visible index cards, computer check-in listings, as well as on catalogue entries. Libraries which do not have a computer programme need not add identifiers or key titles to their catalogue entries.

5. If a computer-based catalogue is basically a record of items in a library; if it is intended to help readers and staff to find those items, then a clear, simple entry will suffice.

Bibliographic records as approved by CONSER are the records which OCLC participants are directed to use for serial cataloguing and for the construction of other files, such as the on-line serial check-in file. Originated at OCLC, the CONSER programme is located in the Serial Record Division at Library of Congress. Other users of this programme are a select group of research libraries.

CONSER records are distributed through MARC serial tapes and LC cards and also through CONSER microfiche.

CATALOGUE FUTURE IN THE NEXT DECADES

Most libraries in US are not closing their catalogue mainly because the present manual entries haven't all been converted and present records aren't all in one standard format.

According to Neal L. Edgar, one summary of future catalogue alternatives collocates material on traditional catalogue forms, machine-readable cataloguing data, computer-supported and on-line interactive catalogues and several comparisons of catalogue formats. The author conclude that, "the form of the catalogue will change, but its function will perforce remain".

Select Bibliography

Collver, M. "Organization of Serials Work for Manual and Automated System. "*Library Resources and Technical Services 24*: 307-16 (Feb. 1980)

Davis, C.C. "OCLC's Role in the CONSER Project". *Serials Review* 6: 75-77 (Oct.-Dec. 1980).

Dunlap, C.R. "Mechanization of Acquisitions Processes." In Advances in Librarianship, edited by M. J. Voigt. new York: Academic Press, 1970.

Gorman, Michael and Robert H. Burger: "Serial Control in a Developed Machine System". *The Serials Librarian*. Vol. 5: 13-26 (Fall 1980).

Mahapatra Piyushkanti, Dr. The computer in Library Service. Calcutta: The World Press, 1985.

Osborn, A. D. Serials Publications: Their Place and Treatment in Libraries. 3rd ed. Chicago: ALA, 1980.

Reddick, J. "Manual vs. Automated Check-In: A Comparative Study of Two Academic Libraries". *Serials Review* 6: 49-51 (Oct. 1980).

Roughton, M. "OCLC Serials Records: Errors, Omissions, and Dependability". *Journal of Academic Librarianship* 5: 316-21 (Jan. 1980).

Rowley, J.E. Organising Knowledge: an Introduction to Information Retrieval. Hants: Grower, 1987.

Serials Automation for Acquisition and Inventory Control. Edited by Gray Potter and Arlene Furber Sirkin. Chicago: ALA, 1981.

Spalding, M. M. "Computer Produced Serials Book Catalog with Automatically Generated Indexes. *Library Resources and Technical Services* 24: 352-60 (Feb. 1980).

Taylor, David C. Managing the Serials Explosion; the Issues for Publishers and Libraries. New York: Knowledge Industry Pub. 1982.

CHAPTER 11

Information Technology And Libraries

WHAT IS INFORMATION TECHNOLOGY?

Information technology (IT) may be defined as 'a combination of computer and telecommunications techniques which makes possible new systems and products to help people at work, in education, and at home'. Information technology is thus all about the application of a wide variety of electronic technologies to the information-handling activities that are central to the operation of any organisation. (Stephen Flowers).

In the domain of library information service, by information technology is meant the use or application of various technologies such as computer, telecommunications, word processing, micrographics, reprographics, video recording and other electronic devices for the storage, retrieval, reproduction and dissemination of information in an office or library environment. While hardware and software, aspects of computer have been discussed in the previous chapters, this chapter reviews host of other technologies and equipment widely used in library operations, or have valid potentials in future.

WORD PROCESSING

Word Processing is a technique for electronically storing, editing, and manipulating text using an electronic keyboard, computer and printer. A dedicated word processors consist of a TV-link viewing screen alongwith a keyboard similar to that of a typewriter, a programmable microcomputer and magnetic floppy disk, and finally a high unit printing unit. However hard disks, and other media such as magnetic tapes and cards are also used in some systems. Regardless of their design almost all word processors have these five components viz a processor (CPU) a keyboard, a display screen or panel removable external storage, and a printer. In fact it is a special purpose microcomputer. However, a general purpose microcomputer can also be used for word-processing if it has sufficient internal and external storage capacity and special word processing software. Mainframe can also serve in the same way.

With the use of simple commands, material typed via the computer keyboard, is stored directly into the computer's memory. Once stored, the information can be reformatted and printed easily via a printer hooked to the computer that receives instructions and then flawlessly types the desired number of copies etc. The equipment also enables users to move words, sentences, paragraphs or whole sections of text, thereby saving enormous amount of retyping times.

Libraries and information centres are greatly benefitted by this machine. The areas of applications are: library catalogues, order processing, periodicals acquisition, abstracting and indexing bulletins, on-line searching, union lists. In addition to this, they are also used for thesaurus construction, database searching, and current Awareness Bulletins etc.

According to James Rice a modern word processing package (whether it is a stand-alone system or is part of a microcomputer system or a time-sharing system has the following capabilities:

1. It is easier to learn the use and does not require technical knowledge.
2. It has many text-editing and formatting capabilities. These include the following:

(a) Right and left margin and right and left indentions of a types of charts, tables, figures can be easily adjusted.

(b) The insertion, deletion, or replacement of letter words, sentences possible. Even paragraphs can be moved and rearranged.

(c) An automatic spelling checks with a large vocabulary provided.

(d) Text input is highly flexible. It means users can continuously keyboard text without regard to carriage returns, paragraph indentions, spaces between lines etc.

(e) Page headings are input once and then automatically repeated on each page.

(f) Pages are numbered automatically.

(g) Line lengths, page lengths are easily formatted.

3. It has the ability to integrate other information from other files into the document being processed.

4. It has the ability to index and retrieve documents that are stored.

5. It has some statistical and computational abilities. It means statistical information might be processed into averages or percentages and then formatted into a chart or table for a specific purpose.

6. It has the ability to converse with the user through terminals.

These are just a few of the fundamental features of modern word processors. They are becoming friendly, easier to use, more flexible, and more powerful all the time. (J. Rice).

DOCUMENT STORAGE AND REPRODUCTION

MICROGRAPHICS

Micrographics is that filed of information technology which concerns making use of microforms. Here copies are produced in a highly reduced formats called microforms such as microfilms, microcards, microfiche, roll films of 8mm, 16mm, and 35mm, micro-opaque, ultrafiche, film strips, insert cards and computer output microform (COM). There are large variety of microforms and reduction ratio ranges from 20:1 to 300:1 or even more are said to be available. Today it is possible to images of thousands of pages on a standard 6" x 4" high density ultra fiche.

Regardless of type, microforms are created in either of two ways. Computer-output microfilm (COM) permits the direct recording of computer processed, machine-readable data onto microfilm or microfiche without first creating paper documents; the second method of microform production called source document microfilming, uses specially designed cameras to film paper documents, recording them as microimages on film or fiche. In either case a COM recorder or microfilm camera produces invisible images which require special reading equipment to be made visible and usable. However latest microform reading equipment making it possible to handle variety of microforms using simple lens changer or adaptor. Roll films in 16mm, 35mm positive and negative microforms, now can be handled with the same reader printer equipment.

Micrographics has enabled libraries to acquire rare material, preserve collections, conserve shelf space, and provide other libraries with copies of scholarly material.

REPROGRAPHICS

The term reprographics is used to identify that field of information processing which concerns with technologies and equipment for the reproduction of documents. Although micrographics can be considered a specialized facet of reprographics, the term is usually applied to copying and duplicating equipment which makes paper copies at or near full size.

While computer remains the nucleus of library automation, copiers and duplicators are historically the most important category of automated equipment in library application.

The electrostatic process in its plain paper (xerographic) and coated paper (elictrofax) still remain the dominant copier technology. The latest plain paper copier Xerox-9500 can give two copies per second. This invention has increased the information transfer process and is regarded a boon in the area of information technology.

Copying and duplicating machines continue to improve capabilities. Photostat machines are available for two-sided copying, reduction and enlarging copying and colour copying. Automatic paper feeding and sorting of multiple copies of multipage documents and automatic stapling of copy sets are widely used in libraries.

Recently computer technology has further influenced document reproduction system. Potentially most important development has been the introduction of so-called intelligent copier, a microprocessor-controlled device which can function as both a conventional copier and an output device for data prepared by computers and word-processing systems. Using a combination of lasers and xerography to generate paper copies, intelligent copiers are related to the high-speed nonimpact printers. These new devices can perform two-sided printing, automatic sorting and automatic stapling. An interesting feature of intelligent copiers is their ability to print characters in multiple type fonts, sizes and intensities. In addition to functioning as conventional copiers, or computer printers, intelligent copiers can create new documents by merging information from existing paper documents with machine-readable data prepared by a computer or word-processing system. (Saffady).

EXPERT SYSTEMS

Expert systems represent one of the most advanced facets of information technology. Basically expert systems are software packages aimed at providing expert consultancy advice and assistance with problem solving in specialist fields of knowledge.

The British Computer Society's glossary defines an expert system as "a computer system containing organized knowledge so that it can perform some of the functions of an expert human consultant". Expert systems are in fact intelligent computer applications that use data, a knowledge base and a control mechanism to solve difficult problems which demand significant human expertise for their solution. They are the best known form of Artificial Intelligence.

Expert systems differ from the conventional computer programs in that they keep separate the knowledge needed to solve problems from the methodology for doing so. The control strategy is maintained at a level distinct from the knowledge base.

The direct application of expert systems to information work has been primarily in the area of online bibliographic database searching. It is predicted that in future the researchers will be able to conduct comprehensive and successful online literature searches without the help of a librarian or information specialists.

THE TECHNOLOGY OF ONLINE SERVICES

During the last 20 to 25 years several kind of data processing and telecommunications technologies have evolved. They have made online information service fast, cheap and attractive. Computer and data processing industries provide the hardware whereas telecommunications industries provide the low-cost data communication links between the user and the computers. (Detail follows under the caption "Telecommunication Aspects") Landau, Wanger and Berger have identified the following major technologies that have contributed to the success of online information services:

1. Powerful time-sharing computers
2. Machine-readable databases
3. Fast-access disc storage devices
4. Interactive retrieval programs
5. Fast, low-cost computer terminals
6. Telecommunications networks

Time-sharing Computers

The modern (fifth-generation) computers are high-speed, have high capacity, for great storage, and data processing capabilities than their earlier (first-generation) ancestors. They too have greatly increased time-sharing capabilities. It means more people can use their resources at the same time from remote terminals. (Detail follows)

Machine-readable Databases

Databases have been defined in number of ways. These are collections of related textual and/or numeric data in machine-readable form that are processed for computerized publishing and/or electronic dissemination. These databases can be "read" and "understood" by a computer only as they are in a binary form.

An online information service essentially acquires machine-readable databases from database producers or suppliers and converts the data to a format compatible with the retrieval system design. Design specifications are developed for the users to convert programs to transfer information from the supplier's magnetic tapes onto magnetic discs in the prescribed retrieval format.

Fast-access Disc Storage Devices

As discussed in the chapter 4, machine-readable data are stored in several ways such as: punched card, punched paper tape, magnetic tape, drums, discs and in the magnetic core of the central processing unit. Magnetic tape and discs are the most commonly used methods of storage. Floppy disc CD-ROM and erasable disc etc., with unbelievable storage capacity have made online service fast and cheap.

Interactive Retrieval Programs

Interactive retrieval programs provide the means for the online user to get the information on the discs through the computer. Batch searching is not interactive, because it is done on database tapes rather than on discs. The tapes are searched sequentially from beginning to end. Discs only have made interactive retrieval possible.

Interactive retrieval requires an interactive program which enables the user to actively communicate with the database. As each stage the search strategy is typed at the terminal and sent to the computer program, the results are immediately displayed.

Although online retrieval program are "Conversational", the interaction is not quite simple. It is achieved by most retrieval programs through a structured protocol of user commands which the program interprets as instructions to the computer to perform certain operations on the data. And the users have to pay for it.

Low-cost Computer Terminals

The availability of high-speed, low-cost modern computer terminal has made online search service a success. At present a large variety of reliable, lightweight and inexpensive computer terminals is available.

Modern terminals have a typewriter-like keyboard, and typically one of two types of output or display-printing or cathode ray tube (CRT) screen. CRT terminals display output on a television-like screen and are usually used with an attached printer for paper copy.

Telecommunications Networks

Telecommunications networks are designed to handle digital machine-readable data and use telephone and lines, microwaves and communications satellites to transmit data. Networks such as Tymnet and Telenet provide communications links for online services, which in the early days had to rely on standard telephone lines designed for voice, not digital data. These networks rely on small switching computers (nodes) in key cities which permit most users to dial a local telephone number. The node computer then allows the user to access any dozens of online services. (Detail follows).

TELECOMMUNICATION ASPECTS

The purpose of telecommunications is 'to transmit representations of information (signals) between remote locations'. The signal carriers can be electrical, electromagnetic, or since the 1970s, light waves. Optical fibre cables are the medium for transmitting light waves.

The development of telecommunications has a great deal of kinship with that of computer science. In fact much of the equipment is common to both fields. Telephone, television, teletypewriters and terminals are just a few examples of engineering technology where improvements and developments are shared by both telecommunication and computing.

Telecommunications media transmit information in two ways: analog and digital. Analog transmission constitutes a jumble of frequencies which are in a continuous range (sound waves, light waves and temperature etc.) Digital transmission occurs in a stream of bits. The bits are binary digits which form a digital code. Not only can numbers, letters, and special symbols be converted into binary code, but sound, light waves, visuals and voice can also be converted. In fact any type of information can be transmitted in either analog or digital form. Some basic concepts are now briefly explained.

Simplex, Half-duplex And Full-duplex

The cables connecting terminals to a computer are generally of three types. Simplex cables permit transmission in one direction only. Half-duplex cables permit transmission in either direction but not at the same time. It means input must be received by the computer before output can be delivered. Many interactive computer system use full - duplex mode. It means data can travel either direction and simultaneously. In this system when information is input to a computer from a terminal, it is also printed at a terminal by a computer. The transmission both ways is so fast that the terminal prints what users input at virtually the same time it is typed on the keyboard.

Time-sharing Systems

The simultaneous interaction of two or more terminals with a computer system is called time-sharing. Many such systems employ a network of dedicated data grade cables. The OCLC network has thousands of terminals connected on dedicated cables.

Time-sharing is so powerful that more and more computer systems are designed for it. With time-sharing, the user inputs the programme on a terminal and gets virtually immediate feedback while still connected to the computer. Errors can be quickly edited and processing is much faster. Time-sharing is very much like a conversation. There is an interchange of information; questions and answers, back and forth. This system is often called interactive computing. It makes use of great deal of direct access storage, notably disk storage. This enables the computer to store and quickly retrieve information during processing.

Online Vs. Offline

When a terminal is communicating directly with a computer, it is said to be online. This term developed from telecommunications because, when a message was produced and sent in the same operation, the user was online. If the message was input via punched cards or paper tape, and then sent all at once, it would be off-line.

Online processing is often called real time processing. Here the user is working on the problem with the direct access to the computer system.

Terminals

Almost any device that is capable of transmitting or receiving information is regarded as a terminal. Terminals can be remote (from the main computer installation) and a batch or interactive. (Fig. 11.1)

Fig. 11.1 (Terminal)

Batch terminals allow large amount of batch processing. A simple remote batch terminal might consist of a card reader and a line printer coordinated by a control unit. Or it might contain a paper tape reader, paper tape punch, line printer and card reader etc.

Interactive terminals are now more common, and permit the keying in of data, the transmission of data to the control computer and within seconds, a computer response to the data received. A typical interactive terminal comprises either a VDU and its keyboard, and/or a printer.

Intelligent terminals do more than merely transmitting and receiving information. It has been programmed to make logical decisions about the data that it handles. It can usually, examine, edit or validate the data, flag errors etc. It handles routine processing tasks without calling upon the main computer.

Transmission Media

The media that may be used for transmitting data are numerous. Twisted copper wires are used for normal telephone line. Coaxial cable is used in some telephone systems and for radio and TV transmission. Coaxial cables might be used for high quality bulk transmission at high speed. Optical fibres, which carry light waves, representing electrical impulses provide a very wide bandwidth and thus high transmission. It is identified that fibre cables have a bandwidth hundreds of times that of equivalent copper cables. One cable has been used that can transmit over one billion bits per second of information. It is estimated that fibre optics can transmit the entire contents of 30-volume encyclopaedia in one second, which may otherwise take several days using conventional transmission means.

Fibre optics is a technology which is to stay permanently. It has also found its way into computer engineering, reprography and a variety of other applications.

Cable Television

Cable television (CATV) appears to be a popular and cheap method of transmission of information even to home. Cable TV Companies (US) are literally wiring the community using coaxial cables that are capable of transmitting digital data as well as video, voice and facsimile. An extraordinary opportunity is emerging as more home computers are acquired, so that the transmission capability of Cable Television, home computer, and Television receivers can be tied together. Since the Television Companies are required to make at least one channel available for public services, the library has an opportunity to interrelate with this new information service facility.

The potential applications to library and information of Cable Television (CATV) are therefore vast. It is stated that CATV offers public libraries the opportunity to expand two of their traditional services-children work and adult education.

Practically CATV takes the form of a TV camera used in the library to transmit a picture of a page of a reference book, illustration or other material over the cable network. Any user who telephones the library with an enquiry but has CATV facility can be shown material relating to their enquiry on their own television screen at home. Thus the marriage of libraries and television is an exciting and promising.

TELECOMMUNICATION NETWORKS

A data network always consists of host computer systems and remote terminals linked by a number of telecommunications channels. (Fig. 11.2)

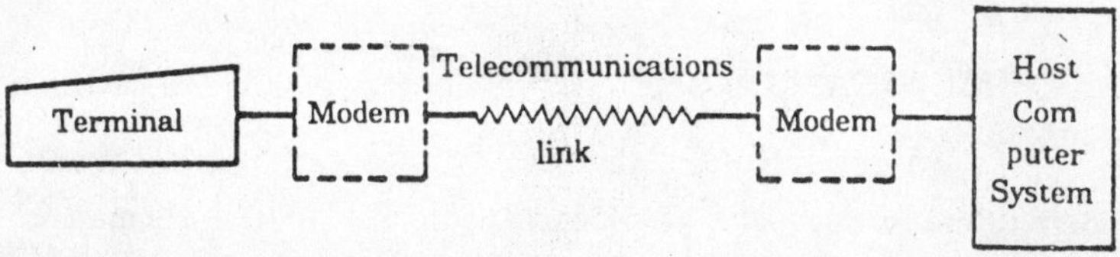

Fig. 11.2 Linking a terminal to a computer system

These data networks have been developed to eliminate the public switched telephone network for carrying of digital information. The notable telecommunications networks are Telenet and Tymnet. These are predominantly North American, but have nodes in Europe, and other parts of the world. These two provides access to nearly all major American hosts. Access to Telenet and Tymnet from Europe is possible via agreements with the national Post, Telephone and Telegraph authorities (PTTs). In the United Kingdom, the International Packet Switch

Stream (IPSS) enables searchers to access computers in North America. IPSS links to Tymnet, Telenet, Uninet and Autonet. Tymnet and Telenet now have many nodes all over the world. Many Arab countries too have access to Telenet, Tymnet, Uninet and Euronet.

Access to hosts in Europe is facilitated by Euronet Diane. A number of European hosts, including BLAISE, Infoline, DIMDI and Data-Star are accessible through Euronet. Euronet also provides links to other European networks. Hosts in Europe can also be contacted through the European part of IPSS network.

Other hosts also have their own networks. Dialog provides Dialnet as a link between California and London. SDC has a line from the USA to its computer in Working. ESA-IRS has Esanet which has a node in London. Most computers bureaux which host the factual databases have their own world-wide networks.

COMMUNICATIONS

To get into the national or international net-works a telephone link is used to access the closest node. Information is transmitted between the terminal and the host computer by direct-dialling or via PTTS in conjunction with data-communications network or via a private leased telephone line. The databases available from the service suppliers are usually accessed over telecommunications network such as Tymnet or Telenet. Communications networks permit terminals to be connected to systems such as DIALOG, ORBIT or BLAISE by dialling the nearest node (i.e. an interchange point) of the network; this usually means a local telephone call to the network number. The user then pays as communication charge from the node to the host. Previously computer link-ups used cables designed to carry the spoken words; now packet-switching technology utilizes networks designed for the transmission of discrete packets of fast data signals via special high-grade paths between computers and terminals.

Information exchange is achieved over the communications network by the transmission of electrical signals in sound waves over the network distances between the user's terminal and the host computer. When the signals are transmitted, the computer's constant-level direct pulses are converted into signals suitable for transmission via telecommunications facilities. The reverse process is performed at the user's terminal. This process is called modulation and demodulation, and the device by which it is accomplished is the electrical coupler the modulator/demodulatior, or modem. (Fig. 11.3 Depicts Communications Processor)

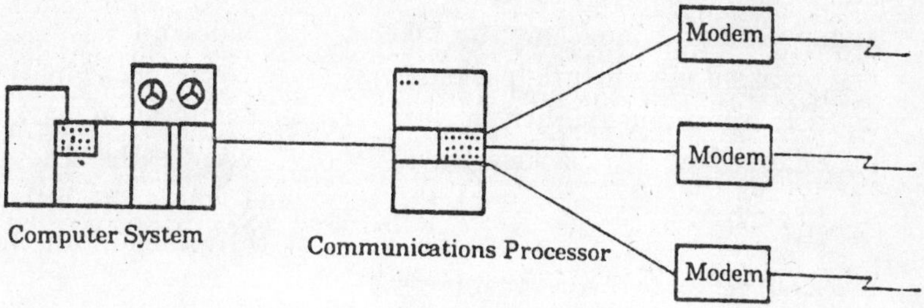

Fig. 11.3 Communications processor

An acoustically coupled modem permits data to be transmitted via the receiver of the standard telephone. This coupler is connected to the terminal by a wired connection, and to the telephone network by an acoustic connection. (Fig. 11.4 An Acoustic Coupler)

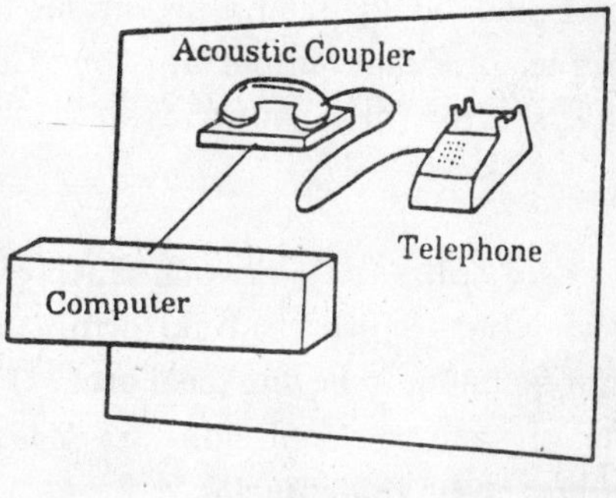

Fig 11.4 (An Acoustic Coupler.)

A modem is permanently wired and converts digital messages i.e. bits which the terminal and computer understand, into analog messages i.e. sound waves, capable of being transmitted down to telephone lines. There is a special type of modem called acoustic couplers which are not permanently wired. These are often used in libraries.

Packet-switching Technique

As stated before, packet-switching system is now widely used. The technique of packet switching consists of breaking up each message in small packets and then switching each and every packet along the quickest communications path available at any instant. A minicomputer takes a thousand-word message and breaks it up into little packets, putting an electronic address on their fronts and another on their tails, as identification mark for each packet. The packets travel down different paths. They all stop at a minicomputer at the other end where the little packets are reassembled on the basis of their identification marks to generate the original message.

British Telecom's Packet Switch Stream (PSS) is designed for the public transmission of data in U.K. and provision is also made for connection to data networks in other countries via IPSS (International Packet Switch Stream) Tymnet which became operational in 1970 is the largest international data communications networks using this technique. Another important one is US-based ARPANET which is serving three countries with 2000 terminals.

LAN

A Local Area Network (LAN) is relatively new type of network which is used to link terminals and computer systems within one building or one local area. Due to close locations high speeds of data transmission are possible. LANs offer great potential use for the libraries.

VIDEOTEX AND TELETEXT

Videotext and teletext were developed as a means of using existing equipment, that is to say, telephones, computers, microcomputers, and television receivers for additional information purposes. But the term 'videotex' was originally suggested by the Comite Consultatif International Telegraphique et Telephonique (CCITT) which is part of the International Telecommunications Union (ITU) responsible for standardization and tariff structures in telephony, telegraphy and data transmission.

Videotex

Videotex is used for a whole class of electronic systems which use a modified television set or a VDU to present computer-based information in a user-accessible visual form. As stated, videotex systems which use telephone lines, or other channels of communications that provide a two-way link, are known as interactive videotex or viewdata systems, whereas videotex systems in which information is broadcast to the terminals, are known as broadcast videotex or teletext systems.

In videotext technology a number of innovative approaches involving various combination of transmission technologies like telephone cable, TV cable, satellite, optical fibres have been recommended for videotext delivery. Personal Computers may become one kind of home terminal device used to approach videotext system. The users could store and interact with the information inexpensively through their home computers. They could get hard copy by using home facsimile or printing devices.

Teletext

Teletext services are broadcast information services which may be accessed in a non-interactive mode. These services may be accessed with a television and a telephone line but tend to be limited in the quantity of information that they can carry. In these systems a sequence of numbered information pages, or screensful of information, is broadcast cyclically over a television channel. The user Keys in the number of the required pages and that page is captured the next time it is transmitted and 'frozen' on the screen.

VIDEOTEXT SERVICES

Britain is credited for generating videotext services (formerly known as viewdata). There are in operation in Britain three videotext services; (i) CEEFAX (BBC), (ii) ORACLE (ITV), and (iii) the PRESTEL. The BBC service is known as CEEFAX and the ITV service is known as ORACLE. All the three services have been developed in Britain as a means of disseminating current information with the help of television equipment with special devices incorporated or attached.

Ceefax and Oracle are quite similar in nature. They involve selection of information by the user, using buttons on the decoder. Each is intended to offer about 200 pages of information-a page being the amount which can be shown on a television screen (920 characters) Colours are used, as are graphic displays. All the information for all the pages is sent by the same channel as is used for the television programmes and simultaneously with them. It is transmitted continuously.

The PRESTEL service is different from CEEFAX and ORACLE services in that its signal is carried from the British Post Office to the User's television set via telephone line; and selection of particular pages of information is made by using the buttons on a push-button telephone.

In PRESTEL, by contrast to CEEFAX or ORACLE, only the information demanded by the individual user is transmitted, and it is transmitted only to him and only for the time he wants. Selection is carried out by computer at the transmission end. In sum, the PRESTEL service system is interactive i.e. the subscriber cannot only receive data from the centre, but also respond to it with replies. But CEEFAX and ORACLE are not interactive services.

The other videotext services worth mentioning are West Law and LEXIS in USA for legal information, the application of CATV (USA) the Florida experiment of USA's Knight Ridder newspaper group, French P&PTIS viewdata terminal for home users replacing telephone directories.

Teleprinter

The teleprinter is to written word what the telephone is to the spoken word. It is a machine on which information is typed, the text is reproduced at a distance on a similar machine. The sending and receiving machines are connected by a telegraph cable or radio. A competent operator can transmit 35 to 40 words a minute. On some machines, the message to be transmitted can be coded on perforated paper tape and then transmitted automatically at 70 words a minute. Incoming messages can also be received in the form of perforated tape for subsequent decoding into printed form.

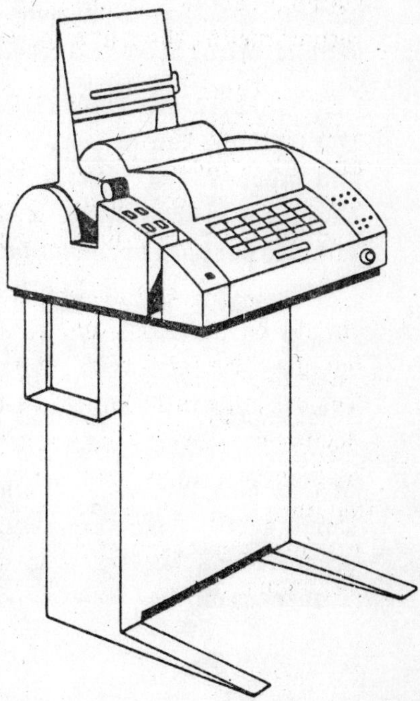

Fig. 11.5 Teleprinter.

A teleprinter connected with the telex network may be left switched on but unattended throughout the day and night. Incoming messages are received and printed automatically - a service of particular importance for international communication between different time zones.

Teleprinters can also be purchased and installed internally for the purpose of communication between departments. They are ubiquitous in big libraries or information centres in industrialized countries and used to transmit reference information quickly and accurately. (See Fig. 11.5)

Telefacsimile

Started in 1948, facsimile transmission is widely used in the libraries of U.S. and elsewhere. This is a system for transmitting visual images by scanning them at a transmitting station, sending them over a communication channel, and reconstructing them at a receiving station.

There are both analog and digital facsimile mechines and facsimile can be sent via cable, telephone lines, microwave and other means. Usually they are sent over telephone lines because it is economical. It takes from a few seconds to a few minutes per page to deliver facsimile documents.

David Heron has emphasized that the telefacsimile should be preferred due to its being faster, less expensive to operate rather than teletype writer manual system. Telefacsimile, also known as facsimile or fax could be used for document delivery. Such a system will provide a copy of a page of text or graphics at a remote location using terrestrial or satellite links. There are a number of national and international organizations beginning to offer fax services. (Fig. 11.6 Fax Transmission)

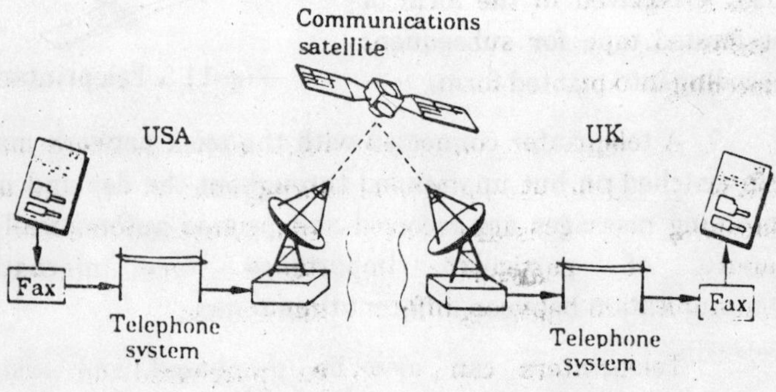

Fig 11.6 (Fax transmission)

Microfacsimile

It refers to the transmission of images on microforms to remotely located places electronically, where they may be received in the form of displays on screen, printed on paper or even in microforms. Thus it links two technologies i.e. facsimile transmission and micrographics to provide one of the useful information transmission systems. One of the recent developments is 'Telefiche'' which consists of four integrated components:

1. A transmitter, called the Telefiche Image Processor, is both a microfiche storage and retrieval unit and a micro-image scanner capable of operating at a maximum resolution of 200 lines per inch. Micro-images are displayed on a rear-projection screen for operation verification prior to scanning. The Telefiche Image Processor's output is a compressed digital signal representing the information content of successive picture elements in the scanned image.
2. A choice of receiving terminals is available. For low volume printing requirements, a Rapifax 100 transreceiver will reconstruct microimage frames as enlarged paper prints at speed ranging from 25 to 90 seconds per frame. For high volume printing requirements, the Telefiche Digital Image Printer operates at a speed of 10 seconds per page (frame).
3. Where hard copy is not desired, a CRT terminal permits the high-speed, full-size display of alphanumeric or graphic images at remote locations.
4. The Telefiche system is designed for use with digital communication facilities.

Teleconferencing

Teleconferencing is a sort of network capability that uses the telephone as a medium for voice transmission, the television for video, and the computer for data transmission service. Data terminals are connected together via the telephone network. Three or more persons working on the same project can communicate with one another through terminals. One participant sends a message to many other participants for comments. Individual responses are appended to the original message and can be reviewed by other participants. These in turn may provoke responses which are themselves made available for review and comment. The result is a recorded dialogue which can be reviewed by all the authorized persons.

Teleconferencing removes barriers of time and geography and allows individuals to participate at their own pace. Donald D. Spencer reports that more than 20 million business meetings are held everyday in the U.S. Those firms which are equipped with proper teleconferencing equipment save travel time and money enormously.

Computerized Teleconferencing

Teleconferencing using audio and video-equipment, as indicated above, requires all the participants to be online at the same time. This more often poses problems. The device computerized teleconferencing permits the participants to attend meetings at their convenience. This is possible because the conference dialogue can be stored in computers.

A computer conference can be seen as something halfway between a conventional conference and a rapidly published newsletters. The system can be used by hundreds of people at diverse geographical locations. Each participant must have an access to a computer terminal connected to the conference network. One can sit at the terminal at a convenient time during the day call up any message and respond to them.

The system has a database containing a large number of text messages. The computer maintains a permanent history of all conference discussion. It remembers which message each user has already seen. When a terminal is switched on by a user, it displays all the entries which have not been seen. The user can directly write his own comments and messages which will be stored in the conference database.

Balagurusamy enumerates a number of advantages offered by computerized Teleconferencing as follow:

1. A person can take part in many ongoing conferences using much less time than for face-to-face meetings.
2. User can read and write at a time suitable to himself or herself.
3. User need not wait for a scheduled time to take up a problem. He can communicate on any day or as and when a problem comes up.
4. Messages are well prepared.
5. Messages of less importance can be skipped.
6. An issue or a problem could be addressed to a large group of people for their comments and suggestions. It is possible to consolidate the suggestions within a day or two.
7. Since it does not involve any travel and stay, it not only saves money but also encourages even less interested people to participate.
8. People with different mother-tongues find it easier to understand written messages than spoken ones. They can take their time to read.

Confravision

The British General Post Office is rendering another service known as CONFRAVISION. It enables meetings and conferences to be held by groups of people sitting in their own offices in various parts of the country. This service indicates the revolutionary changes that communication technology is brining about in all walks of life.

Electronic Mail

The term 'Electronic Mail' has different connotations, but its main characteristics can be said to be the transmission of material from place to place or person to person, using electronic methods of capturing, transmitting and delivering information. As information is visually communicated (not orally) text and graphics can be included and it is not necessary for the information to be in hard copy form. The term covers telex, teletex, packet switching, facsimile, microcomputer communications and electronic mail services. The common feature of all these systems and services is that the messages are converted to electronic signals for the purpose of transmission. Input to, and output from, an electronic mail system can be via a video terminal, or wordprocessor, with printer, a facsimile machine, or any data terminal including computer vision and voice communication systems. Transmission of electronic mail necessitates a telecommunication network.

Most electronic mail subscriber or bureau services have a central computer which operates as a switching centre for 'mail boxes'. Messages are keyed into a terminal and sent to a receiving mail box via telephone lines and a computer. Larger firms are using this to communicate between widely dispersed offices. It too has great potentials for library use.

SATELLITE COMMUNICATION

Another important area of technology is satellite communications which has further reduced the gap between time and space . A communications satellite is launched in a special location 22300 miles above the equator so that its orbit is synchronized to the earth's orbit. Therefore, its position, relative to the earth remains constant. A radio or microwaves signal is then beamed to the satellite, amplified by the satellite, and beamed back to one or more earth stations. The earth stations can then distribute the information via cable, microwave, or any other broadcasting.

As with other telecommunications methods, satellite distribution systems can carry sound, video, and data. There are several cable television systems in U.S. that utilize satellite communications.

Lerner says that 'Satellites can provide instant communications between any points on earth, well beyond the capabilities of land lines or microwave line-of-sight relay systems. The bandwidths available (the bandwidth is related to the amount of information per second which can be passed through communications channel) are far greater than any other available for inter-continental communication. Satellites provide accelerated information delivery at cost which are independent of the distance involved and at speeds ranging from 9600 bits per second to 2,56,000 bits per second (bps). A text page containing 20,000 bits would be transmitted in less than one-tenth of a second'.

Chronologically speaking the first satellite "Sputnik" was launched by Soviet Union on 4th October 1957. The first commercial communication satellite was launched by USA in 1962. Since then a number of communication satellites have been launched by USA. USSR, ESA, Japan, China and India. INTELSAT. (International Communication Satellite Organization) comprises of 109 countries. Its latest generation in INTELSAT-V (two satellites) which can be hired on commercial basis.

Other satellite systems include Canada's TELESAT system using ANIK satellites, Russia's STATIONAR, Indonesia's PALAPA, the French-German Symphonie, Italy's SIRIO. India is probably the seventh nation to have orbited an earth satellite with its own rocket. It orbited INSATIA in April 1982. In Pakistan SUPARCO has planned to orbit a domestic communication satellite (PAKSAT). It will also launch a low orbit scientific satellite 'Badr-A' which will perform four scientific experiments including digital communication. The Islamic Scientific and Cultural Organization (ISESCO) conceived as the virtual UNESCO of the Islamic World must help Islamic Countries in this venture.

Potential For The Future

Satellite combined with other forms of telecommunications such as cable, and facsimile transmission are potentially useful in a wide variety of library applications. Among them are:

1. Remote browsing using slow-scan television.
2. Searching of automated catalogues.
3. Searching of bibliographic and numeric data bases.
4. SDI service.
5. Delivery of documents in real time via facsimile transmitters.
6. Distribution of cataloguing information, e.g. MARC records.
7. National or International-professional conferences without the need for participations to travel great distances.
8. Remote printing of books.

It is maintained that the satellites launched by the USA and the USSR etc are not going to occupy the entire equatorial orbit. There is plenty of room in the equatorial orbit for many more satellites without the danger of collision. It has been estimated that about 22300 satellites could be launched at 22300 miles above a fixed spot on earth.

In USA many believe that eventually electronic information will replace the printed version. Delphic study (US) was conducted posing queries to publishers, librarians and technologists (King et Al. 1981). The following were among the specific forecasts mode:

1. By the year 2000, 50 percent of exiting indexing/abstracting services will be available only in electronic form.

2. Existing periodicals (in science and technology, social sciences, and the humanities) will not reach even the 25 per cent level of conversion until after 2000.

3. By 1990, 25 per cent existing reference books will only be available in electronic form. The 50 per cent level of conversion will only occur after 2000.

4. By 1995, 50 per cent of newly issued technical reports will only be available in electronic form.

F.O.. Lancaster in a way, is a pioneer in the field of electronic publishing. In his latest work "Libraries and Librarians in an Age of Electronics" Lancaster attempts to bring together his extensive writings on evolving technology, the paperless society, and the implications of this evolution for libraries. He reviews the technological trends of the last 20 years in telecommunications and computer technology for applications-such as information storage and retrieval, electronic mail, teleconference, inter-active television, and publishing and forecasts that libraries will use microforms, on-line databases videodiscs, teletext systems or even books or serials on silicon chips to provide their users with the information they need.

It is generally held that the publishers of the "book-on-a-chip" would charge the same price as printed books. Readers would buy them in self-contained "readers" with crystal display or could plug them in to universal readers which would be as portable as the calculator and have the same random access capability as the printed codex book. (Taylor).

Select Bibliography

Adam, Roy J. Information Technology and Libraries: Future for Academic Libraries. London: Croom Helm, 1986.

Advances in Library and Information. v.1 Edited by Dr. C.D. Sharma and Dr. D.C. Ojha. Jaipur: RBSA Publishers, 1988.

Balagurusamy,E. Office Automation and Word Processing. New Delhi: Tata McGraw-Hill, 1987.

cecil, P.B. Management of Word Processing Operations. Reading, Mass: Addison-Wesley, 1980.

Changing Information Concepts and Technologies: a Reader for the Professional Librarian. New York: Knowledge Industry Pub. 1982.

Flowers, Stephen. Success in Information Processing. Suffolk: John Murray, 1988.

James G. Williams. Information Technology: Critical Choice for Library Decision-Makers. New York: Marcel Dekker, 1982.

King, Donald W.,ed. Telecommunications and Libraries: A Primer for Librarian and Information Managers. White Plains, N.Y.: Knowledge Industry Publications, 1981.

Kleinschrod, W.A., Druk, L.B. and Turner, H.J. Word Processing: Operations, Applications, and Administration. Indianapolis: Bobbs-Merrill, 1980.

Lancastr, F.W. Information Retrieval Systems, 2nd ed. New York: John Wiley, 1979.

Mckean, J.M. Facsimile and Libraries; Telecommunication and Libraries: a primer for Libraries and Information Managers. Edited by D. W. King et. al. New York: Knowledge Industry Pub. 1981.

Masterson, William. Information TEchnology and the Role of Librarian. London: Croom-Helm, 1986.

Reynolds Dennis. Library Automation: Issues and Applications. New York: R.R. Bowker, 1985.

Rice, James. Introduction to Library Automation. Littleton: Libraries Unlimited, 1984.

Saffady, W. "Facsimile Transmission for Libraries: Technology and Applications Design", *Library Technology Reports* 14: 445-532 (Aug. 1978).

Salton, Gerard & McGill, Nichael J. Introducion to Modern Information Retrieval. New York: McGraw-Hill, 1983.

Tedd, Lucy A. An Introduction to Computer-Based Library Systems: 2nd ed. New York: John Wiley, 1984.

Telecommunications and Libraries: a Primer for Librarian and Information Managers. New York: Knowledge Industry, 1981.

Vickery, B.C. & A. Information Science in Theory and Practice. London: Butterworths, 1987.

Woolfe, R. Videotex: The New Television-Telephone Information Services. London: Heyden Publishing, 1980.

CHAPTER 12

Automation Planning And Implementation

Library automation in itself, is not a panacea for all sorts of library operational problems. The computer is indeed a sophisticated machine with enormous capacity and capability which can be exploited fully if data and instructions are fed into the machine in the right way. The human factor is therefore not less important in the planning process of computerization than the other factors like selection of the equipment (Hardware) for a specific purpose. The cost-effective analysis is of prime importance which is also inclusive of the human factor. But today, the diminishing cost of the computers, particularly the mini, and the microcomputer and their enormous capability make library automation an economically viable proposition. Further the computerization necessitates a set of situations, a volume of preconditions such as trained personnel, a long-term planning, properly trained end-users, or as a whole what may be called, the computer environment.

SYSTEM AVAILABLE

For library automation, several different computer systems for varied kind of applications are available. The latest trend in United States and elsewhere is to establish an in-house integrated computer system. Many libraries are acquiring their own small computer (mini or micro) and using it for a variety of purposes. This is happening particularly in small libraries. In some cases such libraries use standard software packages whereas some other prefer to develop their own special programs. For developing small background study, some most important computer systems are reviewed in this section.

1. A Transferred System

By a transferred system means where a library, instead of developing its own computer system, just adapt a system being used in another library. This process involves transferring the software developed at one library to another library. A library may choose equipment from competing vendors as already developed or buy a turnkey system, the same one as used for another library.

A transferred system software developed by another library may be attractive in terms of cost-generally the cost of reproducing the computer programs on magnetic tape plus the costs of photocopying the system documentation. There is also a good deal of help available from the library or vendor who has offered the system. By adapting another library's systems, many cooperative possibilities may result between the libraries as a by product.

Transferred systems are usually provided by Book-jobbers or COM vendors or those agencies which are offering online search systems.

2. Turnkey Systems

The turnkey system is a complete system, installed by a vendor on the library's premises. By turnkey means, the library just turns the key and the system operates. The vendor of turnkey systems supply the hardware and complete packaged software and is responsible for dealing with any problems in the system.

In the turnkey system the library staff could make the desired changes on the assumption that they possessed the necessary experience and qualifications. The most common examples of turnkey systems at present are minicomputer based integrated library system. They perform almost all housekeeping jobs as an integrated unit.

3. In-house Development

Instead of buying ready made turnkey systems, the library can develop its own in-house integrated online library system or may use the computer of its parent organization. Before the advent of vendors of automated systems, this was the only way to obtain a system.

In-house (local) system can be tailored to meet the specific requirements of the library. The library can maintain and improve it more easily than with some other types of systems. If the system is developed in a timesharing environment instead of on its own stand-alone computer, costs can be reduced, since the library does not have to buy its own computer hardware. Locally developed systems are very costly as the library needs to engage systems analysts programmers and other consultant. There is also a danger that locally developed system may not work at all.

The computer of a library's parent body is usually large general purpose mainframe equipment. This option is available particularly to large libraries or university libraries. But it is not recommended for the majority of libraries because of the high failure rate among libraries. This solution looks cheap in that it does not cost the library "real" money. But it carries great problems in that the computer and the programming staff are not under the control of the library and thus it has to compete with other departments for the necessary computer system resources.

COMPUTER BELONGING TO EXTERNAL SERVICES

A number of computer-based online library services are available in the United States and Europe. Prominent among them are Bibliographic Utility (e.g. OCLC, RLIN, WLN) and UTLAS, BLAISE, LASER. Jobber/Vendor services such as EBSCO (US) Faxon (US) Swets and Zeittinger (Netherlands) Blackwell's Oxford (UK) offer variety of online services to libraries subscribing to them. These external services usually assist in installing and maintaining essential computer hardware in the library and also help in training the library staff to operate and manage the system.

FEASIBILITY STUDY

Before any computer system is installed in the library a formal study should be undertaken to ascertain the feasibility of the new system. This study should not be carried out by one person alone but by a team including some librarians and other people with relevant computer expertise.

One of the first steps in feasibility study is to establish the information needs and ideal objectives of the system. It will help determine utility of the computer replacing manual system. It is often desirable that the members of the project team may visit other similar types of library operating computer-based systems similar to that being investigated. The visits might give more insight into the equipment involved and how it works. The comparative study would reveal success or failure of the computer systems in operations enabling the visitors to make judgment and determine which system will suit their purposes.

It is also essential to identify the manufacturers of suitable hardware, software or turnkey system and the suppliers of services. It is recommended to put the products to demonstration during feasibility stage so that their suitability can be assessed. This is the stage where potential benefits are identified and an estimate of the likely costs determined.

SELECTION CRITERIA

The library administrator should take into consideration the following points in an attempt to select the suitable computer system to be introduced in the library.

1. Whether the library is going to install its own independent computer system or will it be a member of computer network? (if available).

2. Whether the library will use a mainframe computer or a distributed system with several mini or micro computers? This is for a large organization of which library is just a part.

3. Whether the general-purpose or the specific purpose computer system will be developed? Also whether general application or special application software will be developed?

4. Whether library automation will be made as an integrated total system or partially work unit by work unit?

5. What will be the relation between the routine jobs, i.e. acquisition, cataloguing, circulation, serial control, etc. and storage and retrieval of bibliographic information?

6. What will be the procedures of information transfer and data processing? (Mahapatra)

All these factors need to be discussed and decision taken on a particular system design. On the basis of the assessment report, the particular computer system of a particular firm should be selected after carefully studying the system, its programming, the software applications, conversion, and implementation, review of the system and the structured approach to the system development.

SURVEY REPORT

The preliminary survey report should contain the following:

1. A short description of the present system.

2. The needs of the library and the current trends in library automation, providing a solution and at least one alternative method.

3. A description of further work required before implementing decision.

4. The implications and applicability of the lesson learnt from other computer-based library systems.

5. The procedures of operations and kinds of services appropriate to the library.

6. The cost of the present library system and outline costs of the proposed computer system.

7. The benefits of the new systems qualitative and quantitative as much as possible.

8. Responsibilities of the library staff, implication for staff levels, space requirements and institutional policy.

9. The essential computer orientation of library personnel, adaptability to the new situation and subsequent study up to implementation. It may also include accommodation and location of the computer system, air-conditioning, electrical installation, and telephone connections to be provided etc.

Before implementation phase starts, it is necessary to obtain approval from the library's management/advisory committee in the light of the survey report.

The formal feasibility study is important because it provides the sound footing, the right psychological environment for both positive and negative attitudes to the possible application of computer to library operation.

PARTIAL OR INTEGRATED SYSTEM

It is vitally important for the library to decide whether to start with a partial approach, i.e. computerising by piecemeal work unit by work unit or wholly from the very beginning. A number of turnkey systems are available which are sufficient for single work unit such as circulation or acquisition work etc. But presently there is a clear trend away from automating bits and pieces or single subsystems toward integrated systems in which all library subsystems such as acquisition, circulation, cataloguing are interrelated and share a common database. (Fig

12.1 illustrates an Integrated System) It is therefore more advisable that instead of buying a turnkey system or independently buying software and hardware, the library in Pakistan may develop its own integrated online library system inhouse. It has been stated earlier that at present a number of Turnkey systems suppliers have developed a multiphased or integrated online system for libraries which can perform all housekeeping jobs.

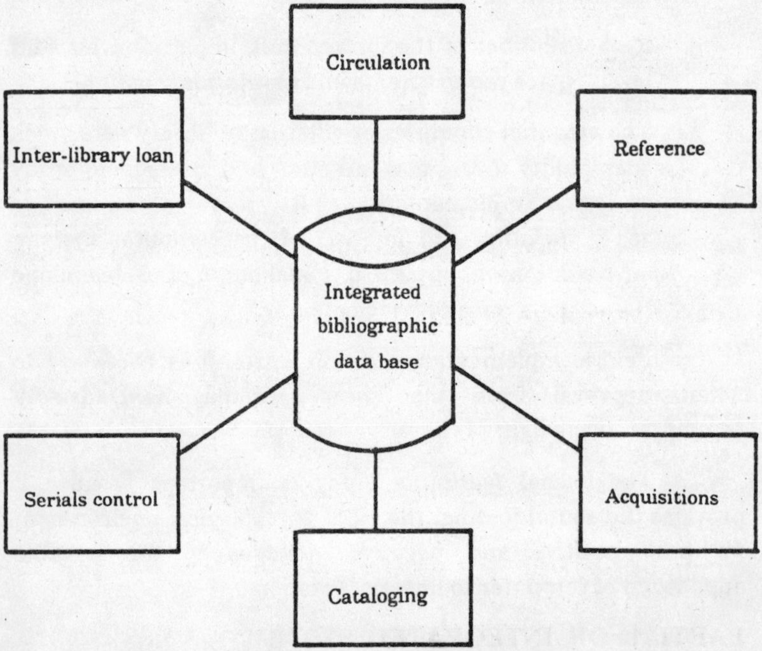

Fig 12.1 (Integrated Library System)

INDIVIDUAL OR INTEGRATED COMPUTER SYSTEM

Another vital area of planning decision concerns two different approaches to library automation. The first one is that computerization may be introduced individually enabling the library to do its all housekeeping jobs and bibliographic storage and retrieval without external interference. Or, secondly the library may become a unit of an integrated computer system for all of its functions just by getting interconnected with an outside computer system through communication channels and the information network. The library has to choose (in U.S.) either of the two approaches. But simultaneously it is possible to start with the individual system and then get connected with an integrated national system to become one of its constituents. (Mahapatra).

In Pakistani situation libraries may adopt a single specific job-oriented system designed for circulation or acquisition etc. But such job-oriented systems have become outdated and not liked by the users. Moreover, it has been experienced that library jobs overlap each other and there is every possibility of sharing data in each of those jobs. For example acquisition data, cataloguing data, and bibliographic data are more or less identical. The serials control data may be used for current awareness service. Bibliographic data may be used for selective dissemination of information service. Thus any computer system adopted in a library may be so designed as to become an integrated Online system comprising all the jobs from the very beginning. The planning and designing of such a system in a Library will have great potentials and promise for future expansion of library services.

SOME SERIOUS IMPLICATIONS

Tedd and many other analysts like Richard DeGennaro have reviewed the implications of introducing automated library systems which the planners and library administrators must keep in view before implementation. It is important to keep the following general caveats when considering whether or not to automate:

1. A good manual system is almost invariably better than a haphazardly implemented automated system.
2. Merely putting a function on the computer will not clean up a poorly thought-out procedure. In fact it will probably make it worse.

3. Not every task worth doing is worth automating.

4. Automation almost never eliminates any jobs nor is it a money saving device.

5. Computer does not make everything effortless. It warrants a lot of spade work (coding etc.) before it is introduced.

6. It is not easy to transfer the programs for computer-based systems between libraries.

7. It is not cheaper to share computer services or join networks.

8. It is highly expensive to maintain manual records of the library during the switchover period but it is indispensable. It will cost much more if the new system fails and the library is left without any usable records.

9. It is not possible to settle for half-automation and half-manual records. Libraries cannot take full advantage of automation until they can implement integrated systems and they cannot have integrated systems while a substantial portion of their records is on cards in traditional catalogues.

10. Retrospective conversion of the library records to machine-readable form and consolidation of all the bibliographic records into a single integrated system is highly costly, labour-intensive and time-consuming. But it is a must for a complete successful automated library operation.

METHODS OF IMPLEMENTATION

As soon as it has been decided which system is to be used the job of converting library records from the existing system to the appropriate form and format for the new system should be initiated as early as possible. A number of alternative methods of conversion exist including:

1. Outside service bureau: A paper or microfilm copy of the shelflist of the library is given to the service bureau. They in turn transform this information into machine-readable form on keypunched cards, tape etc. In U.S. a number of commercial firms specialize in data conversion.

2. MARC. Various cataloguing services, such as OCLC, RLIN, WLN, UTLAS provide compatible MARC database for the generation if required of local bibliographic record. It increases the possibility of finding the item already catalogued. If not available the library can enter the catalogue data for the item in hand.

3. A contract can be made with a book jobber or a COM catalogue company to provide a full MARC record, on magnetic tape for each item in the collection.

4. In-house project. This approach is expensive in terms of staff-time, equipment and programming changes, but it is the only feasible method in countries like Pakistan.

Apart from this there are many other alternatives available in U.S. or Europe. For instance, online conversion is possible via local terminals to a bibliographic database obtained from a commercial source loaded in the library's minicomputer. The same system and process can be obtained from another library and used likewise.

Whichever type of solution has been adopted it is essential to test fully the computer system introduced. The hardware installed needs to be checked to see if it is working satisfactorily before the software is loaded and tested. In Pakistan where libraries evolve their own programs, these must be designed, documented and tested so that they efficiently meet the requirements of the organization.

For computerising of housekeeping routine, a library may attempt partial or integrated online system, but it must be done in a planned way. It may be implemented according to the library's own situation. Tedd has recommended the methods of implementation which might include:

1. **Phased Program.** In this approach the total system is divided into sections and each section is installed individually and proved to work satisfactorily before another section is installed.

2. **Parallel Programs.** The manual and automated operations may continue parallel for a period of time until it has been proved that computer system works satisfactorily. By this method day to day work is not disturbed.

3. **Complete Change Programs.** Partial or integrated system may be designed and implemented completely; then it comes into operation on and from an appointed date. Once the changeover is made to automated operation, there is no going back to the old manual system.

The final aspect of the implementation stage is the maintenance and development. If a software package, a turnkey system or the services of a specialist supplier or cooperative has been chosen then arrangements for maintenance and acquisition of enhanced versions of the system should have been made with the supplier (Tedd). If program has been specially written for in-house use, i.e. locally developed software, then however well designed and tested, it is quite likely that changes will be required after the said software has been used for a while. It is also possible that library service itself might change, demanding consequent change in computer programming.

TRAINING OF STAFF

The training of the Library Staff is crucial for the success of an automated system. The amount and type of training, however depends upon the functions the various library personnel will perform. But it is vitally important that each member of the staff be given a general orientation about the new system. They must be well-conversant with the online search and information retrieval methods with a sufficient knowledge about the needs of end-users. The Managers holding key positions at different levels with specific job assignments must be trained adequately and their training should be updated periodically. It is considered a good idea to appoint a particular member of the library staff responsible for the training and retraining if necessary within the library and to keep up to date with developments in the system being used.

It is strongly recommended that when the system is ready for use and before implementation all the circulation staff must be specially trained to understand the new automated system. Moreover, all the staff should be provided with clear, readable, and accurate documentation for the new system. It is quite advisable that when the system is operational and staff are well proficient in using it, a demonstration to the total library staff be given before implementation. Public relations policies, user services, etc. can be reviewed and handouts intended to explain the system to the users might also be introduced to be staff at this time.

Poor or insufficient training may cause poor relations between people and the computer. It is also feared that inadequate training may generate bad feelings and negative attitudes about the automated system leading to a failure.

INTRODUCTION TO THE LIBRARY USERS

Automated systems in the Libraries are adopted solely with the intention to provide improved services to their users. So it is very important that library users should know of these. It is also essential to record how the users react to the automated system.

Techniques for introducing or promoting new or improved services to users might include producing an informative leaflet, arranging for an article to be written in a local newspaper, organizing displays at suitable exhibitions and running general demonstrations (Tedd).

EVALUATION

Setting up an automated system in a library, apart from technology change, brings about a number of other changes. For instance, the library services changes, user's needs change, staff activities change, and library's own environment and reputation changes. Also a computer system, having planned, designed and implemented is likely to be superseded in the years to come by some new system. It is therefore important for the library manager or administrators to monitor and evaluate the system after it has been in operation for six months to a year so that any modification or improvement could be made where appropriate at right time.

Joseph R. Matthews suggests that evaluation process should not be completed by those associated with the implementation of the system, but instead completed by other library personnel or a consultant. James Rice proposes to form a committee of frequent users of the system and the project manager. J.R. Matthews recommends that the postimplementation evaluation should too seek to determine whether the system was delivered as defined in the contract and the contractual obligations of both the parties have been adhered to. It is also necessary to compare actual costs and benefits with those estimated before the implementation of the system.

How well the automated system is accomplishing its intended purpose can be determined by carrying out a survey of the various library personnel engaged in the operation. At this point it is essential to interview them to ascertain their level of satisfaction with the system itself and with their training and orientation. It is a right time to ask them for any suggestion or improvements that would make their job easier and the system a success.

Users should also be asked to evaluate the new system. A brief evaluation form can be developed with the users in mind and they can rate the system using a rating scale. (J. Rice).

Possible benefits that may be derived from a postimplementation evaluation are: a revised and strengthened maintenance contract with the system supplier, identification of possible modifications that will improve library operations, possible changes in the manual procedures that interface with the automated system, and some improvements in the work flow of the library slightly altering the physical arrangements (J. R. Matthews).

Select Bibliography

Bierman, Kenneth John. Automation and the Small Library. Chicago: Library Administration and Management Association, American Library Association, 1982.

Corbin, John. Developing Computer-Based Library Systems. Phoenix, Ariz: Oryx Press, 1981.

DcGennaro, Richard, "Libraries and Networks in Transition: Problems and Prospects for the 1980s". *Library Journal 106*: 1048 (May 15, 1981).

Hayes, Robert. Consulting in Computer Applications to Libraries. *Library Trends* 3: 381-98 (Winter 1980).

Lovecy, Ian. Automating Library Procedures: a survior's handbook. London. The Library Association, 1984.

Mahapatra Piyushkanti, Dr. The Computer in Library Service. Calcutta: The World Press, 1985.

Matthews, Joseph R. Choosing an automated Library System: A Planning Guide. Chicago: ALA, 1980.

Reynolds Dennis. Library Automation: Issues and Applications. New York: R.R. Bowker, 1985.

Rice James. Introduction to Library Automation. Littleton: Libraries Unlimited, 1984.

Taylor, David C. Managing the Serials Explosion; the Issues for Publishers and Libraries. New York: Knowledge Industry Pub. 1982.

INDEX